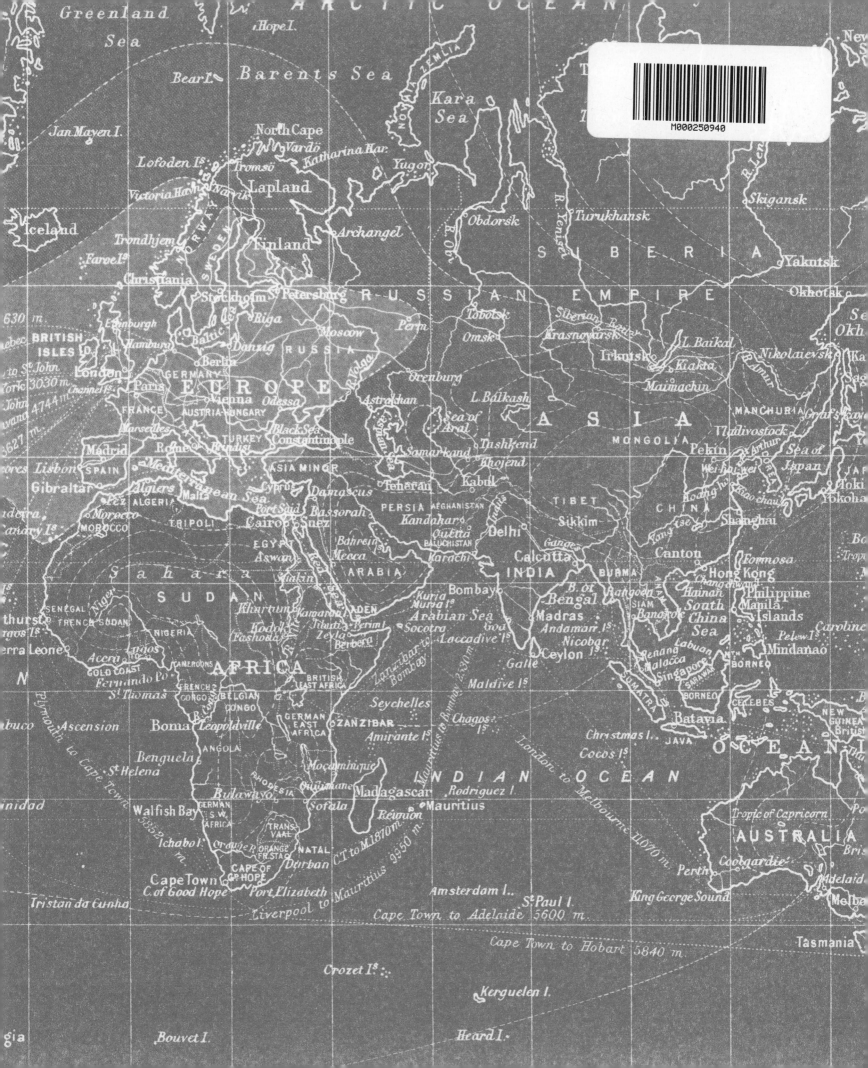

Royal Geographical Society

with the Institute of British Geographers

THE
MAP TOUR

ROLEX

Rolex supports the Society's Collections, contributing towards their conservation and helping to secure public access and inspire new uses of one of the world's pre-eminent geographical archives.

THIS IS AN ANDRE DEUTSCH BOOK

Royal
Geographical
Society
Enterprises
Commercial activities
supporting the charity
The Royal Geographical Society
(with the Institute of British Geographers), London

Published in 2018 by André Deutsch Limited
A division of the Carlton Publishing Group
20 Mortimer Street
London W1T 3JW

A CIP catalogue for this book is available from the British Library.

ISBN: 978 0 233 00556 0

Printed in Dubai

Royal Geographical Society

with the Institute of British Geographers

THE
MAP TOUR

Hugh Thomson

ANDRE
DEUTSCH

Contents

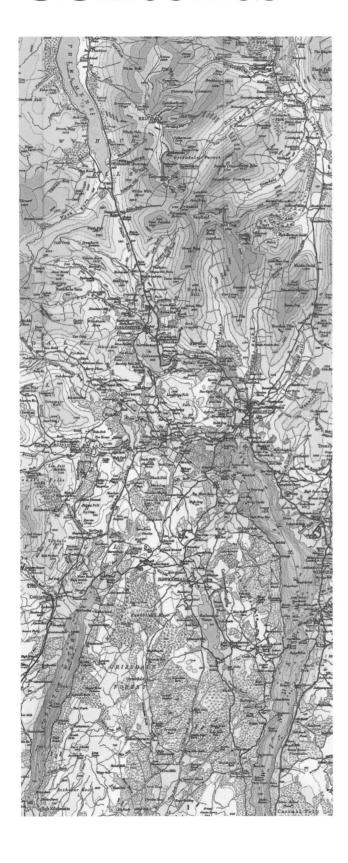

Introduction

There have been many books in the past about pioneers like Columbus, Cook and Vasco da Gama, as well as the maps that were drawn up as the known horizons of the planet expanded.

This volume is different. These wonderful maps from the Royal Geographical Society's Collections were made for the many travellers who wanted to see the world without necessarily having to do it as part of an expedition; who in fact quite enjoyed the comforts of an inn or the availability of a railway.

One could say that these maps were designed to entice the viewer to a known world rather than tentatively to outline the boundaries of a new one.

Rather than explorers, I have taken as my touchstone for the accompanying text those best travel writers of their generation who wanted to encourage as many people as possible to follow in their footsteps: from Boswell and Johnson in the eighteenth century, right up to John Steinbeck in the twentieth century.

In the same way that a path is created across the face of a mountain – first by a few adventurous souls finding their way, then by the many who follow and confirm that it is the right one – so too it often was with travel in the centuries following the Grand Tour.

The enterprising Victorian businessman Thomas Cook led the charge in the later nineteenth century, determined that as many people as possible should be able to experience the pleasures of places like the Holy Land and Switzerland, which had always seemed remote and inaccessible before.

By 1878, Mark Twain, that indefatigable American traveller, was staying at a hotel in the Bernese Alps near the Jungfrau and the Eiger, and reflecting:

What a change has come over Switzerland, and in fact all Europe, during this century. Seventy or eighty years ago Napoleon was the only man in Europe who could really be called a traveller; he was the only man who had devoted his attention to it; he was the only man who had travelled extensively; but now everybody goes everywhere; and Switzerland, and many other regions which were unvisited and unknown remotenesses a hundred years ago, are in our days a buzzing hive of restless strangers every summer.
(Mark Twain, *A Tramp Abroad*, 1880)

By 1907, another seriously energetic American traveller, Hiram Bingham, could encourage his fellow countrymen to visit South America, which few had done as tourists before; his own discovery of Machu Picchu a few years later was to do much to turn the first trickle into the millions of foreign visitors who visit Peru and South America today.

Researching this "Traveller's Atlas" has proved a fascinating task. I had no idea that the Holy Land enjoyed such a boom in British visitors after the first consulate was opened in 1839; that goats and sheep still roamed the Colosseum when British aristocrats visited it for the Grand Tour (Boswell remarking on the ordure they created); or that Afghanistan was promoted as a tourist destination in the 1960s.

I hope that readers can enjoy the wonderful range of opportunities that these maps from the Royal Geographical Society's world-class collection represent; and that maybe it may entice them to make more journeys of their own.

Hugh Thomson

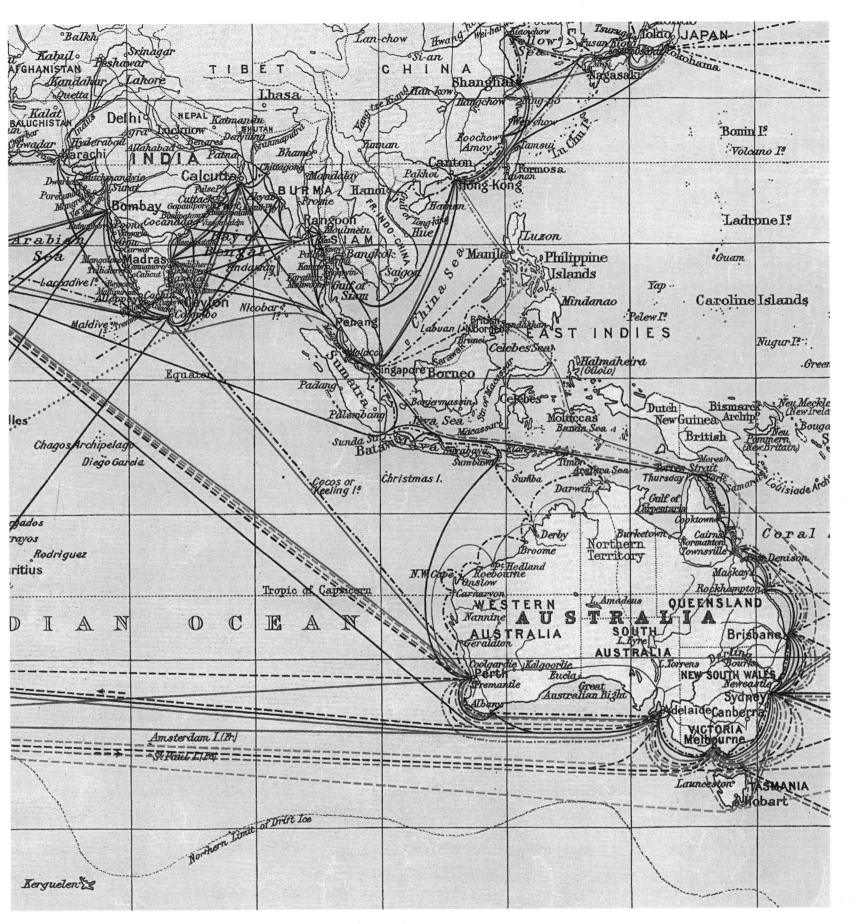

Above: Detail from "World Traffic System of the P&O: British India, New Zealand, Union and Associated Liner". J. Bartholomew & Son, 1930.

I

Cultural Travel

1680–1810

Right: "France, Divided into its Generalities with Adjacent Coasts of England, Holland, Ireland, Spain, Portugal". By Thomas Jefferys, 1756.

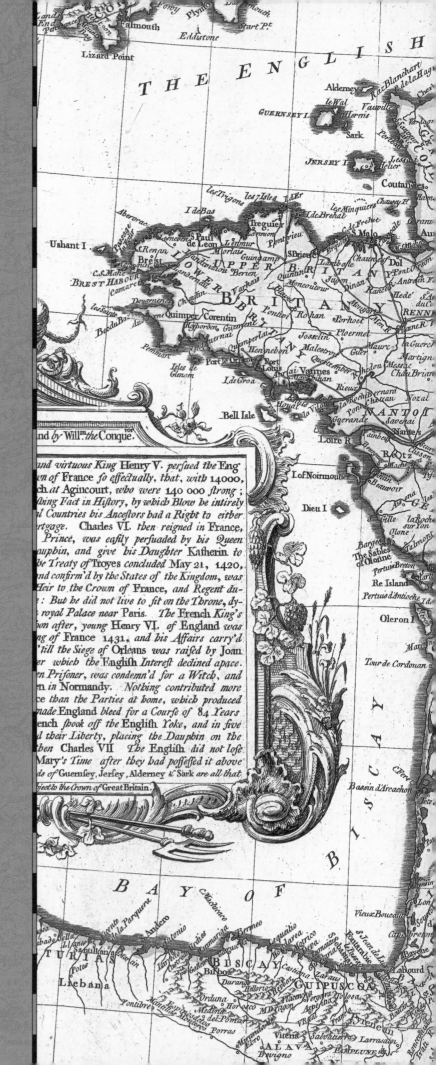

and by Willm the Conque.

and virtuous King Henry V. persued the Eng
wn of France so effectually, that, with 14,000,
ch at Agincourt, who were 140 000 strong;
fing Fact in History, by which Blow he intirely
al Countries his Ancestors had a Right to either
rtgage. Charles VI. then reigned in France,
Prince, was easily persuaded by his Queen
auphin, and give his Daughter Katherin to
be Treaty of Troyes concluded May 21, 1420,
nd confirm'd by the States of the Kingdom, was
Heir to the Crown of France, and Regent du-
: But he did not live to sit on the Throne, dy-
royal Palace near Paris. The French King's
on after, young Henry VI. of England was
ng of France 1431, and his Affairs carry'd
'till the Siege of Orleans was raised by Joan
er which the English Interest declined apace.
en Prisoner, was condemn'd for a Witch, and
n in Normandy. Nothing contributed more
ce than the Parties at home, which produced
nade England bleed for a Course of 84 Years
ench shook off the English Yoke, and in five
d their Liberty, placing the Dauphin on the
then Charles VII The English did not lose
Mary's Time after they had possessed it above
ds of Guernsey, Jersey, Alderney & Sark are all that
ject to the Crown of Great Britain.

CHANNEL
GULF OF LIONS
PICARDY
GENER. OF AMIENS
NORMANDY
CAUX
GENER. OF ROUEN
ISLE OF FRANCE
GEN. OF ALENCON
CHAMPAIN
GENERALITY OF CHALONS
LUXEMBURG
LORRAIN
METZ
ALSACE
MAINE
BEAUCE
ORLEANOIS
GENERALITY OF ORLEANS
SOLOGNE
TOURAINE
ANJOU
BERRI
GENERALITY OF BOURGES
NIVERNOIS
BURGUNDY
FRANCHE COMTE
BRESSE
POITOU
GENERALITY OF POITIERS
LA MARCHE
BOURBONNOIS
GENERALITY OF MOULINS
AUVERGNE
LIMOSIN
GENER. OF LIMOGES
ANGOUMOIS
PERIGORD
LYONOIS
BEAUJOLOIS
FOREZ
VIENNOIS
DAUPHINY
SAVOY
SWITZERLAND
GENEVA
Lake of Geneva
VALAIS
PIEDMONT
PROVENCE
LANGUEDOC
CEVENNES
GENER. OF MONTAUBAN
AGENOIS
BAZADOIS
ARMAGNAC
ASTARAC
GENER. OF BOURDEAUX
GUIENNE
CONSERANS
Mouth of the Rhone
Road of Marseilles
Road of Toulon
The Hieres or Golden Isles
Paris
Rheims
Troyes
Dijon
Besançon
Lion
Grenoble
Avignon
Marseilles
Toulon
Toulouse
Bourges
Orleans
Tours
Limoges
Nevers
Moulins
Clermont
Montpellier
Narbonne
Nimes
Arles
Aix
Strasburg
Mentz
Treves
Luxemburg
Turin
Geneva
Chambery

A Tour of the Whole Island of Great Britain

One historian of the seventeenth century, Christopher Morris, has commented that by the time this map (opposite) was published, "the British were becoming highly immodest about their own political achievements, their own great man, or 'worthies', their own architecture and landscape and, above all, their own prosperity."

This was reflected by the maps and travel books that were produced at the time, to satisfy this renewed curiosity and pride in their own country. Many prosperous households would have displayed a copy of Camden's *Britannia*, an erudite survey from the previous century. But there was clearly a need for a more up to date guide and this was provided by the finest chronicler of Hanoverian England, Daniel Defoe, whose *Tour Thro' the*

Whole Island of Great Britain was published anonymously in three volumes between 1724 and 1726.

The work purports to be a journey right around the country – "the Whole Island" of the title. But Defoe is, of course, best known as a novelist and there was considerable literary artifice to this supposedly journalistic account of his travels around Britain. As one biographer has pointed out, during the period when he was supposedly taking his tour, "it is doubtful whether he ventured further afield than London, Tunbridge Wells, when he took the waters, and Colchester where he had a farm." Instead, he relied on his substantial journeys in the past for what was really "a voyage through his memory and imagination".

Above: "The Roads of England According to Mr. Ogilby's Survey", 1700.

Opposite: "Parade, Tunbridge Wells". Illustration from *Colbran's New Guide for Tunbridge Wells* … Edited by James Phippen, 1844. "Tunbridge wants nothing that can add to the felicities of life, or that can make a man or woman completely happy, always provided they have money." Daniel Defoe

A master storyteller, Defoe presents a fascinating portrait of England as it was in the decades after this map was printed.

He began his literary journey in Essex, where he claims that such was the unhealthiness of the Essex marshes, there were men who had been through up to 14 or 15 wives, all of whom had died:

The reason, as a merry fellow told me, who said he had had about a dozen and half of wives, (though I found out afterwards he fibb'd a little) was this; that the men always went up into the hilly country for a wife. When they took the young lasses out of the wholesome air, they were healthy, fresh and clear, and well; but when they came out of their native air into the marshes

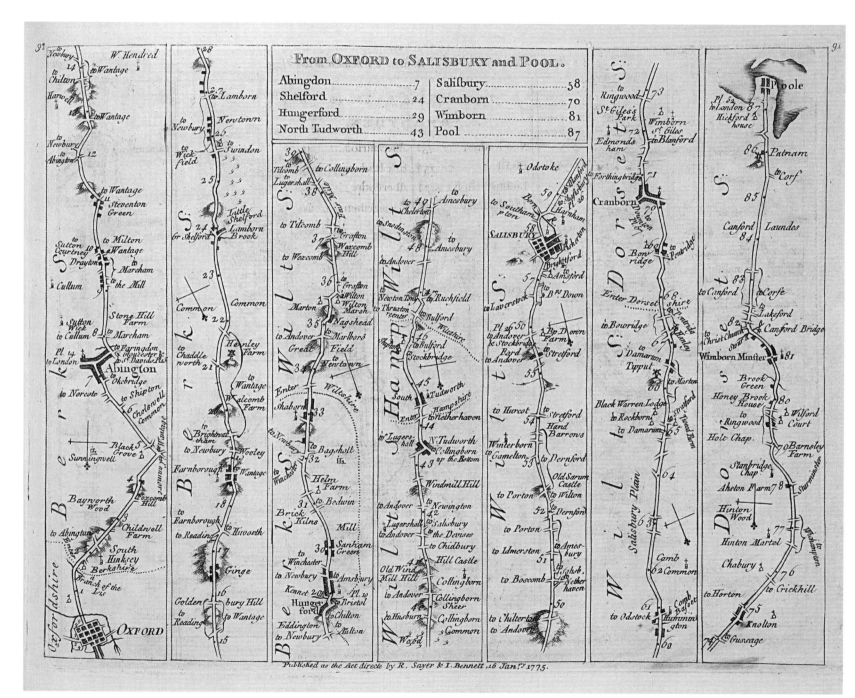

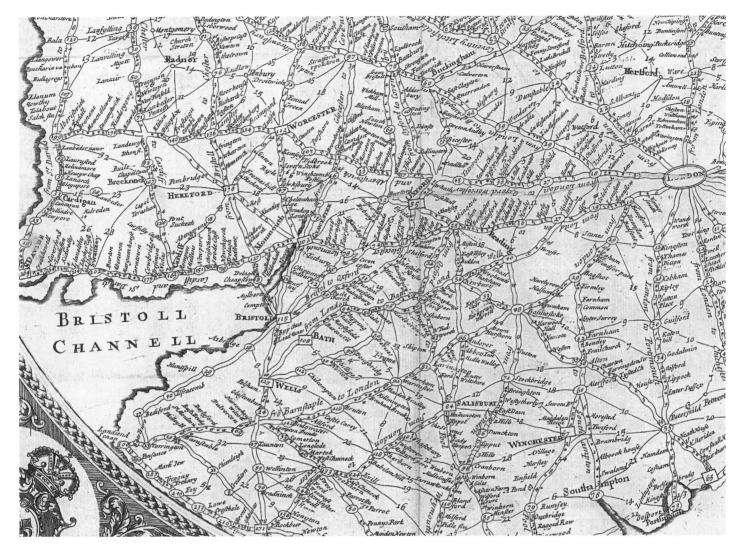

Opposite: "From Oxford to Salisbury and Pool". Plate from *Jefferys's Itinerary; or Travellers Companion, through England, Wales, and Part of Scotland*, 1775.

Above: Detail from "The Roads of England According to Mr. Ogilby's Survey", 1700.

among the fogs and damps, there they presently chang'd their complexion, got an ague or two, and seldom held it above half a year, or a year at most, [before dying]; and then, said he, we men go to the uplands again, and fetch another wife!

Defoe's account of the country is bracingly contemporary. He has little interest in what he describes as "antiquities" – indeed, he often berates cathedral towns, not least because, as a Puritan, he disapproved of what he saw as their papist origins. Even Oxford and Cambridge interest him little.

He is far more concerned with commerce and with the beginnings of what was to become the Industrial Revolution by the end of the century. He notes with approbation where trade is flourishing, and with disdain where communications or roads are poor.

At Dunwich on the East Coast in Suffolk, he is amazed by how the once thriving herring port had decayed and was now almost completely submerged by the sea. "The ruins of Carthage, or the great city of Jerusalem, or of ancient Rome, are not so wonderful to me," he proclaimed.

He is a keen observer of agricultural practice; that, for instance, farmers in Suffolk have begun to feed their sheep and cattle on turnips, while lamb in Dorset has a particularly sweet taste because of the good quality of the grass. In Norfolk he notices that there are a great number of pheasant, which he ascribes to there being far more tradesmen than gentlemen, as otherwise they would have been shot.

This tart description of Tunbridge is typical of Defoe's occasionally acidic tongue: "Tunbridge wants nothing that can add to the felicities of life, or that can make a man or woman completely happy, always provided they have money; for without money a man is no-body at Tunbridge, any more than at any other place." But he is also capable of rhapsodizing about a scene like this on the "delicious" North Downs near Epsom:

When on public race days they are covered with coaches and ladies, and an innumerable company of horsemen ... and then adding to the beauty of the sight, the racers flying over the

course, as if they either touch'd not, or felt not the ground they run upon; I think no sight, except that of a victorious army, under the command of a Protestant King of Great Britain could exceed it.

He appreciated eating fine oysters at Poole, pilchards near Dartmouth, and the fine quality of the beer in the north of the country; while at Wellington in Somerset he was heckled by beggars after he mistakenly gave some change to a few, which "brought such a crowd of them, as if the whole town was come out into the street and they ran in this manner after us."

In his novel *Moll Flanders*, he made the famous observation about Bath that it was a city "where a man may find a mistress, but very rarely look for a wife". Progressing onwards to Bristol, he notes how it has a stranglehold on all trade with Ireland, although he presciently predicts that Liverpool may come to be a rival.

The hills and mountains of Wales alarmed him, as they did many contemporary travellers, and while he described

Aberystwyth as "a very dirty black smoky place", he looked more favourably on Pembroke and Cardiff.

Travelling through Derbyshire, he remarked, patronizingly, that the greatest wonder of the county was why a palace as magnificent as Chatsworth was built in a place where no one would ever see it. After passing Manchester, "the largest village in England", he visited the tomb of Edward I near Carlisle to complete his tour of England and Wales; perhaps fittingly, if not tactfully, as Edward I, "the Hammer of the Scots", had also subdued Wales by force.

Defoe had been a strong supporter of the Act of Union, which united England and Scotland in 1707, and his tour promoted the idea of a country which, as he put it in his preface, was "the most flourishing and opulent in the world".

Opposite: "The King and Queen's Baths, Bath". Illustration from *The Spas of England, and Principal Sea-bathing Places*, by A. B. Granville, 1841. "Where a man may find a mistress, but very rarely look for a wife."

Right: "The Roads of England According to Mr. Ogilby's Survey", 1700, detail. Defoe noted with approbation where trade was flourishing, and with disdain, where communications or roads were poor.

Below: "Chatsworth". Illustration from *England Illustrated, Or a Compendium of the Natural History, Geography, Topography, and Antiquities Ecclesiastical and Civil, of England and Wales*, 1764. "Why was a palace as magnificent as Chatsworth built in a place where no one would ever see it?" asked Defoe.

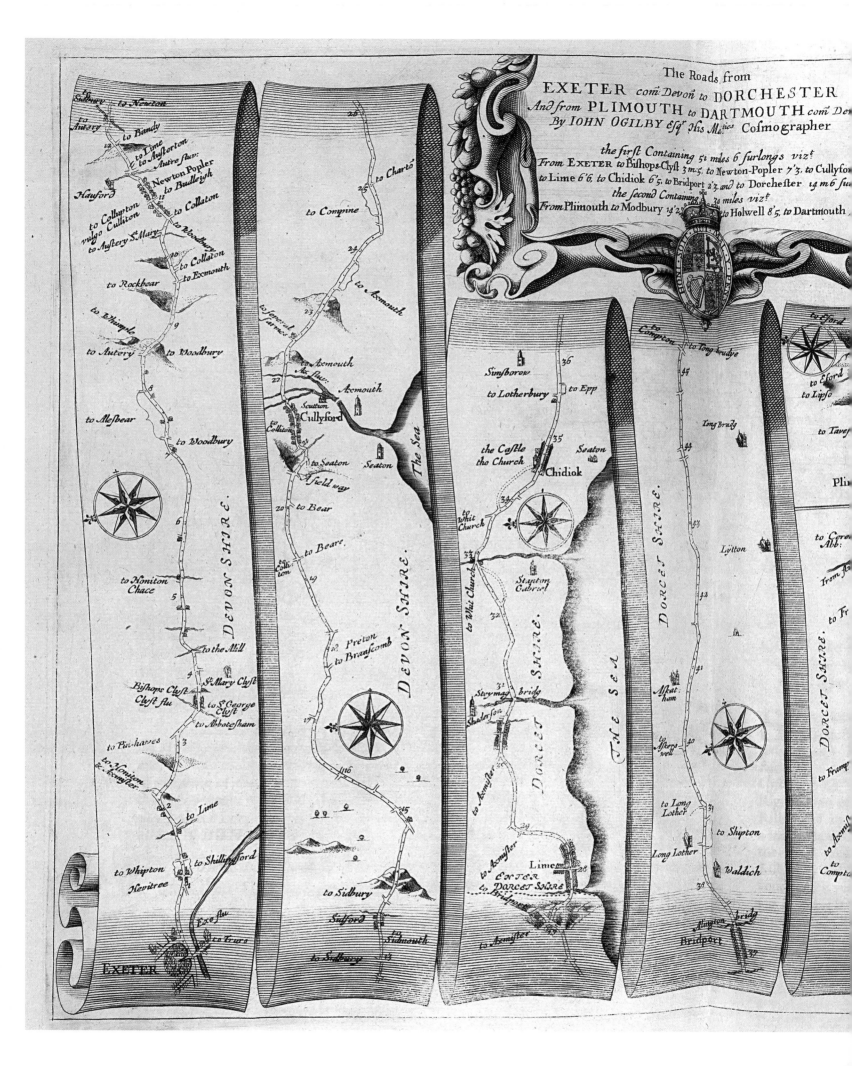

The Roads from
EXETER com̄: Devoñ to DORCHESTER
And from PLIMOUTH to DARTMOUTH com̄ Deu
By IOHN OGILBY Esqr His Maties Cosmographer

the first Containing 51 miles 6 furlongs vizt
From EXETER to Bishops-Clyst 3 m̄:5. to Newton-Popler 7'3. to Cullysfor
to Lime 6'6. to Chidiok 6'5. to Bridport 2'3. and to Dorchester 14 m 6 fu
the second Containing 30 miles vizt
From Plimouth to Modbury 14'2 to Holwell 8'5. to Dartmouth

DEVON SHIRE

DEVON SHIRE

DEVON SHIRE

DORCET SHIRE

DORCET SHIRE

DORCET SHIRE

DORCET SHIRE

The Sea

THE SEA

EXETER

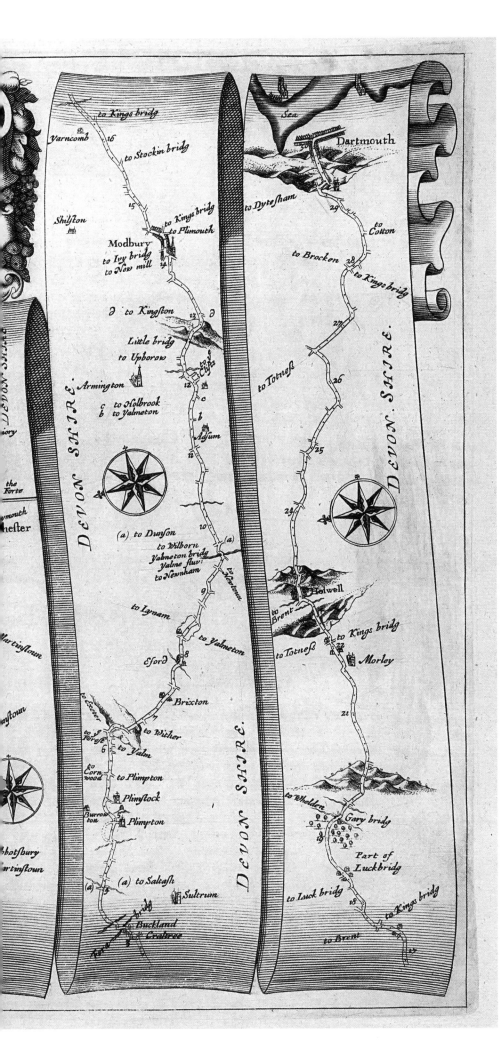

Left: "The Roads from Exeter ... to Dorchester and from Plimouth to Dartmouth". Plate from *Britannia, Volume the First, or, an Illustration of the Kingdom of England and Dominion of Wales: By a Geographical and Historical Description of the Principal Roads thereof ...* by John Ogilby, 1675.

The Western Isles

Dr. Johnson had for many years given me hopes that we should go together and visit the Hebrides. Martin's account of those islands had impressed us with a notion that we might there contemplate a system of life almost totally different from what we had been accustomed to see; and to find simplicity and wildness, and all the circumstances of remote time or place, so near to our native great island, was an object within the reach of reasonable curiosity.

So begins James Boswell's *Journal of a Tour to the Hebrides,* which he published in the year after his friend Samuel Johnson's death, 1785.

It is one of the most striking of all eighteenth-century travel books, not least because some 10 years before, Johnson had published his own account of the same journey, *Journey to the Western Islands of Scotland,* so we have parallel accounts of the same events. Given the great differences in their character – the sober and bear-like Dr Johnson compared to the excitable and febrile Boswell – this can be both amusing and illuminating.

Both men had been drawn to the Hebrides in Scotland by themselves reading a travel book when they were much younger. "Martin's account", mentioned by Boswell in his opening lines, was *A Description of the Western Islands of Scotland* by a native of the Hebrides, a man called Martin Martin, published in 1703. Dr Johnson told the story of how his own father "had put Martin's account into his hands when he was very young".

As with many travel writers travelling in the footsteps of someone else, his influence on their journey did not prevent them from patronizing and denigrating their predecessor. Johnson considered that because Martin lived in the Hebrides, he did not realize how extraordinary the society there was, because he had no point of comparison; while Boswell commented sniffily that "his book is a very imperfect performance. Yet as it is the only book on the subject, it is very generally known ... [However,] I cannot but have a kindness for him, notwithstanding his defects."

This contemporary map (pp.20–21) would surely have whetted their appetites – although it is noticeable that the "prospects" displayed to accompany it are all of city centres, not of the wilder island scenery that the romantic sensibility would so come to admire later in the century.

Boswell passes off airily the potential hazards of visiting these remote parts of the British Isles: "We reckon there will be some inconveniences and hardships, and perhaps a little

Above: Samuel Johnson. From *The Life of Samuel Johnson*, 1897.

Opposite: Title page from *A Description of the Western Islands of Scotland* by Martin Martin, 1716. Both Johnson and Boswell had been drawn to the Hebrides by reading Martin's travel book when they were younger.

Following pages: "New Map of Scotland ... with the Roads and Distances Mark'd Down", 1732. A George Grierson copy of a Herman Moll map.

A
DESCRIPTION
OF THE
Western Islands
OF
SCOTLAND.

CONTAINING

A Full Account of their Situation, Extent, Soils, Product, Harbours, Bays, Tides, Anchoring-Places, and Fisheries. The Antient and Modern Government, Religion and Customs of the Inhabitants; particularly of their Druids, Heathen Temples, Monasteries, Churches, Chappels, Antiquities, Monuments, Forts, Caves, and other Curiosities of Art and Nature: Of their Admirable and Expeditious Way of Curing most Diseases by Simples of their own Product.

A Particular Account of the *Second Sight*, or Faculty of foreseeing things to come, by way of Vision, so common among them.

A Brief Hint of Methods to improve Trade in that Country, both by Sea and Land.

With a New MAP of the Whole, describing the Harbours, Anchoring-Places, and dangerous Rocks, for the benefit of Sailors.

To which is added, A Brief Description of the Isles of *Orkney* and *Schetland*.

By M. MARTIN, Gent.

The SECOND EDITION, very much Corrected.

LONDON,

Printed for A. BELL at the Cross-Keys and Bible in Cornhill, T. VARNAM and J. OSBORN in *Lombard-Street*, W. TAYLOR at the Ship, and J. BAKER and T. WARNER at the Black Boy in *Paternoster-Row*. M.DCC.XVIII.

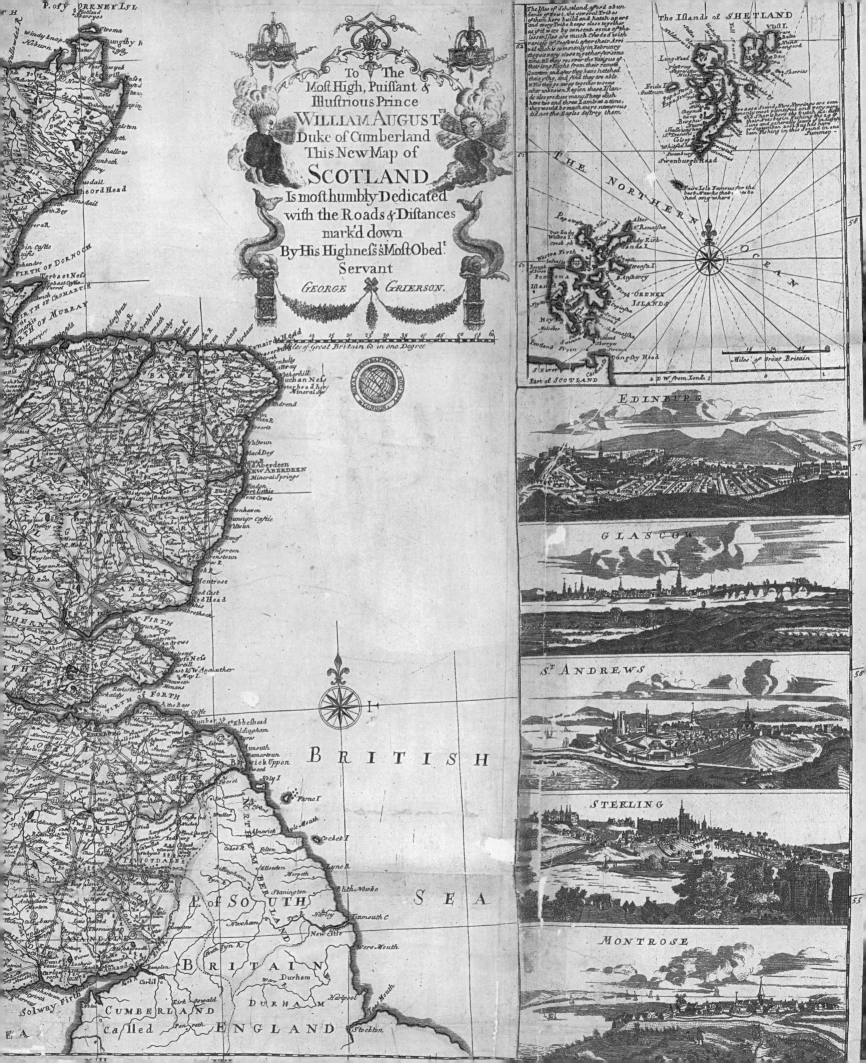

To The
Most High, Puissant &
Illustrious Prince
WILLIAM AUGUSTUS
Duke of Cumberland
This New Map of
SCOTLAND
Is most humbly Dedicated
with the Roads & Distances
mark'd down
By His Highness's Most Obedt.
Servant
GEORGE GRIERSON

The Islands of SHETLAND

THE NORTHERN OCEAN

ORKNEY ISLANDS

Part of SCOTLAND

Miles of Great Britain

EDINBURG

GLASCOW

St. ANDREWS

STERLING

MONTROSE

BRITISH SEA

ENGLAND

BRITAIN

CUMBERLAND

Solway Firth

Durham

danger; but these we were persuaded were magnified in the imagination of everybody."

A great name-dropper, Boswell tells the reader that he had mentioned their proposed Hebridean journey to Voltaire when he had met him in France. Voltaire had looked at him "as if I had talked of going to the North Pole". With the sort of detail that Boswell always relished and that makes him so readable, he noted that the conversation had to be in French, because Voltaire could not talk English without putting his tongue between his teeth, which he had lost.

So in the late summer and autumn of 1773, Johnson and Boswell began their 83-day journey through Scotland, concentrating on the Western Islands in particular. The resulting narratives are very different. It is sometimes said that while Johnson tried to describe Scotland, Boswell spent most of his time trying to describe Johnson. His account of their journey prefigures his great biography of Johnson, which came some years later.

Some mistakes in the cartography are reminders of how imperfectly the islands of Scotland were still known. The orientation of Skye, for instance, is completely wrong. There are some charming comments and footnotes, particularly where the mapmaker may have felt he was on unsure ground when it came to giving actual place names. So, for instance, we learn that "a great quantity of herrings are caught in the bays of Skye" and that "Stornoway Castle was destroyed by an English garrison kept by Oliver Cromwell".

However, there is a further and more sinister hinterland to this map. The dedication by the mapmaker George Grierson is to William August, Duke of Cumberland, better known to posterity as "Butcher Cumberland" for his role, infamous in Scotland, at the Battle of Culloden in 1746 and its aftermath. The youngest son of George II, Cumberland pursued the Jacobites under Bonnie Prince Charlie to Inverness, where the battle of Culloden played out on a boggy field that gave the English the advantage. Cumberland showed no mercy to the defeated Jacobites, and then began a savage clearance of the Highlands.

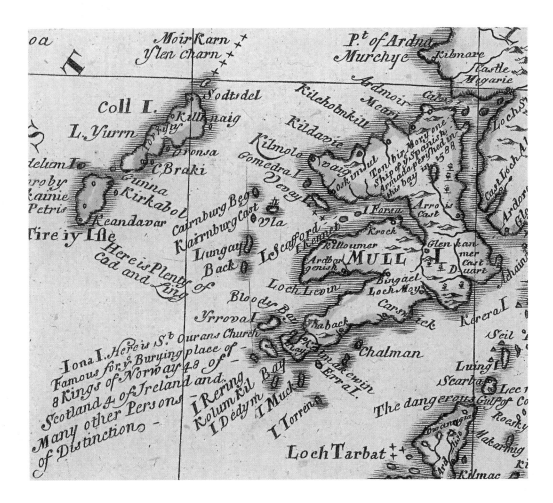

While he was widely admired back in England for his achievements – especially by his Whig supporters – he was equally reviled in Scotland. This map would have found few purchasers north of the border.

Charles Edward Stuart, "Bonnie Prince Charlie", escaped from Culloden and sought refuge in the Western Islands before sailing for France. Johnson and Boswell, who both had Jacobite sympathies, enjoyed tracking down traces of his escapades there in 1773 when they made their journey. In particular, they tracked down Flora MacDonald, who had helped save the Prince some 27 years before.

Boswell took great relish in telling the story of how Flora MacDonald – now a "little woman, of a mild and genteel appearance, mighty soft and well bred" – had then disguised the Prince as her maid, "Betty Bourke", although she added that the Prince "looked somewhat awkward in women's clothes". In this way, she had smuggled him from the Outer Hebrides to Skye on a small boat.

Samuel Johnson's account of their journey has the freshness of a man who had very seldom travelled out of London. His enquiring mind found much to digest – although again, like many a traveller, he feared he had come too late and that the old ways of the Highlands had already changed irrevocably.

Given that Boswell had the first word, perhaps Johnson should have the last. He said of Scotland that "the country consists of two things, stone and water. There is, indeed, a little earth above the stone in some places, but a very little; and the stone is always appearing. It is like a man in rags; the naked skin is still peeping out." And with perhaps more sympathy, he also commented that "of what they had before the late conquest of their country, there remains only their language and their poverty."

Above: The Isle of Skye (left) and the Isle of Mull (right). Details from "New Map of Scotland ... with the Roads and Distances Mark'd Down", 1732. A George Grierson copy of a Herman Moll map.

Following pages: "Fingal's Cave in Staffa". Plate from *A Tour in Scotland, and Voyage to the Hebrides*, by Thomas Pennant, 1772.

The South Sea Bubble

Herman Moll was the most important cartographer working in England during the early eighteenth century and this work was part of his *The World Described, or a New and Correct Sett of Maps*, published in London as a set in 1726, although this particular individual map (pp.28–29) would have been prepared some years beforehand.

During his long career of over 50 years, Moll developed an elegant style that blended accurate information with a picturesque sensibility, much in the manner of many of the writers that he associated with, like Jonathan Swift and Daniel Defoe, or the antiquarian William Stukeley. He was part of a circle which congregated at Jonathan's Coffee House at Number 20 Exchange Alley, Cornhill, London – a place well known because it was where shares were also traded, most notoriously those of the South Sea Company, whose bubble was to burst so spectacularly.

Moll had earlier produced "A New & Exact Map of the Coast, Countries and Islands within ye Limits of ye South Sea Company" (1711) and this map of South America, probably first produced in 1712, would have been viewed with interest by his coffee house clientele, given that the South Sea Company was given a monopoly to trade with South America. His clients needed to have accurate and impartial information about the world to make commercial decisions, just as did his political patrons – like the map's dedicatee, Charles Spencer, Third Earl of Sunderland, the son-in-law of the Duke of Marlborough.

Sunderland had considerable influence at court, although this diminished after the fiasco of the South Sea Bubble. Because of his involvement in launching the scheme of 1720, he was held accountable for it and tried before the House of Commons, so that in 1721 he resigned his offices, and died in the following year, 1722.

Left: Detail from "Map of South America, According to the Newest and Most Exact Observations", by Herman Moll, *c*.1726.

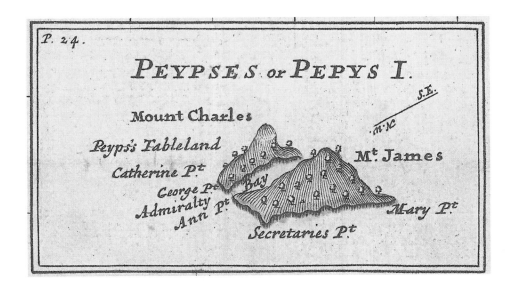

Something of the tone of the coffee house circle comes across in the furious note that Moll has added in the middle of the South Atlantic, which begins, "The world is in nothing more scandalously imposed upon than by maps put out by ignorant pretenders who most falsely and impudently assume the title of the Queen's geographers."

He continues by excoriating certain "falsely projected French maps" which were then on the market. He makes the telling point that these mistakes resulted in the sailing distance to the South Seas appearing to be 1000 miles less than it really was – a crucial commercial consideration for any trade. The tone could

be that of his friend Jonathan Swift, who mentions Hermann Moll's maps by name in *Gulliver's Travels*.

The strength of Moll's invective against these rival cartographers is perhaps weakened by his own inclusion of a completely mythical island – the so-called "Pepys Island", which

Above: Pepys Island. Detail from "A New & Exact Map of the Coast, Countries and Islands within ye Limits of ye South Sea Company", by Herman Moll, 1711. A phantom island, which almost certainly had been caused by a mistaken sighting of the Falklands to the south.

Below: Detail from an advertisement for *The World Described: or, a New and Correct Sett of Maps*. A George Grierson copy of the Herman Moll atlas, 1732.

Following pages: "Map of South America, According to the Newest and Most Exact Observations", by Herman Moll, *c*.1726.

Juſt Publiſh'd by *George Grierſon* at the *King's Arms* and *Two Bibles* in *Eſſex-Street*. Dublin.

The WORLD deſcribed:

OR, A

New and Correct Sett of MAPS.

SHEWING.

The KINGDOMS and STATES in all the known Parts of the Earth, with the principal Cities, and moſt conſiderable Towns in the World: Wherein the Errors of the ancient *Geographers* are corrected according to the lateſt Obſervations of Travellers, as communicated to the *Royal Society* of *London*, and the *Royal Accademy* of *Paris*, by HERMAN MOLL, Geographer. Each MAP is neatly engraved on Copper and printed on Two Sheets of Elephant-Paper; ſo that the Scale is large enough to ſhew the chief Cities and Towns, as well as provinces, without appearing in the leaſt confus'd. And to render theſe MAPS the more acceptable, there is engraved on ſeveral of them what is moſt remarkable in thoſe Countries.

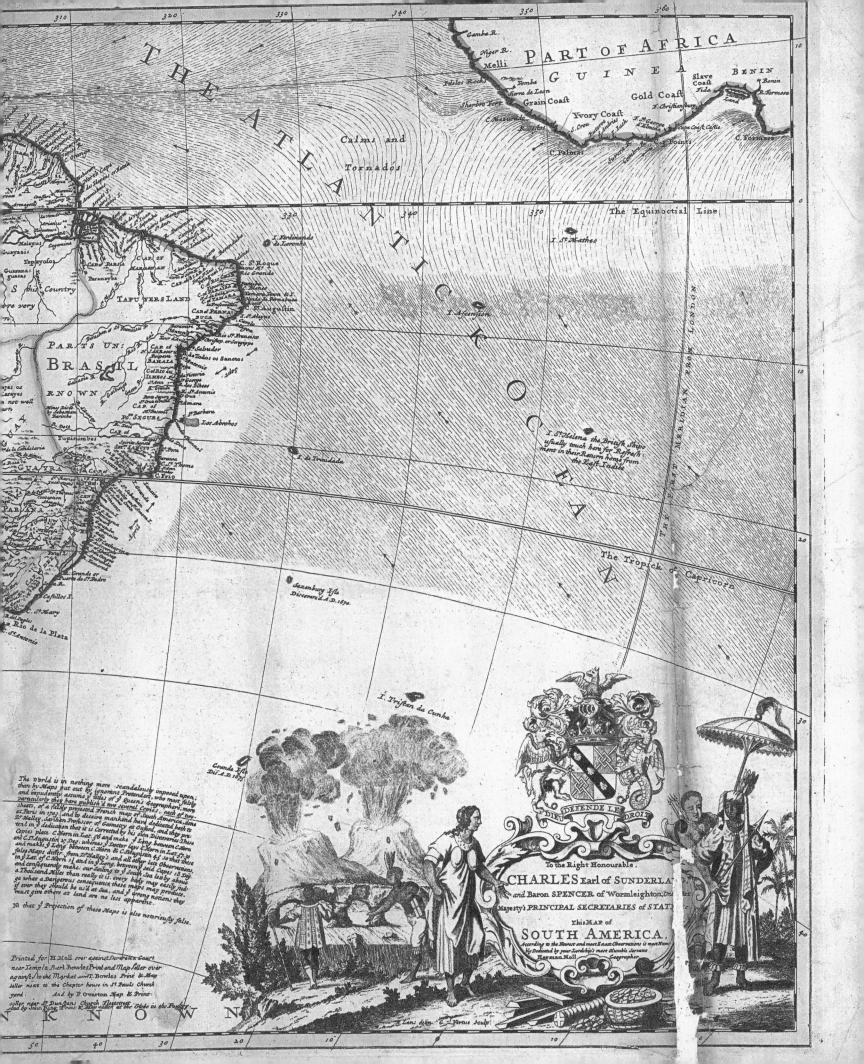

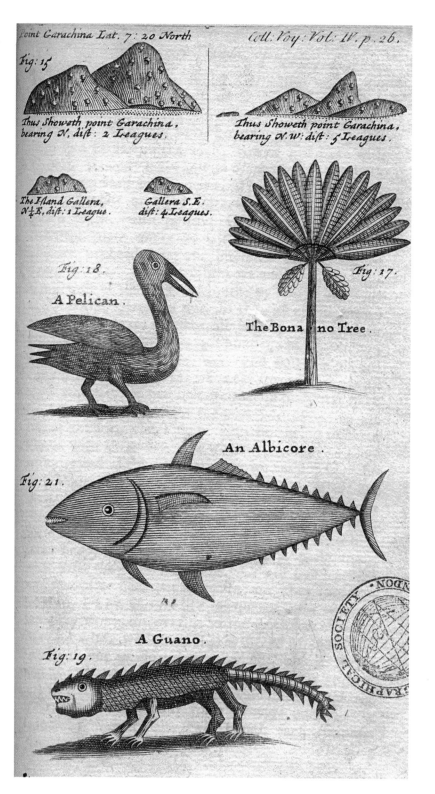

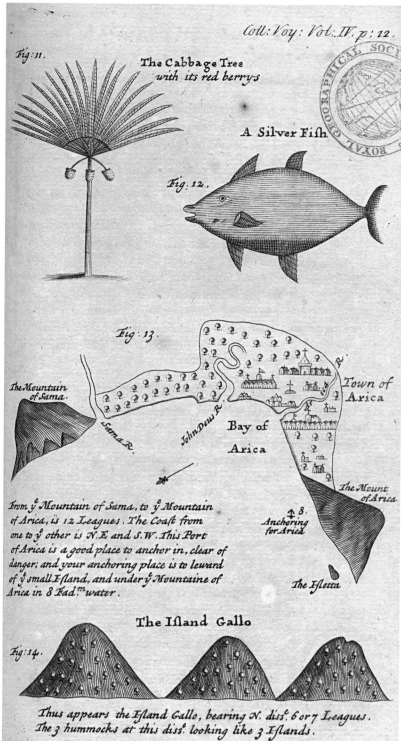

Above: Plates from *A Collection of Voyages*, by Captain William Dampier, 1729.

Opposite: Captain William Dampier (1652–1715). Dampier's A *New Voyage Round the World* of 1697 was a tremendous success that helped inspire interest in South America.

he claims was discovered in 1684 and places just to the left of his rubric and above the Falklands.

Perhaps because of its inclusion in what was seen as one of the most accurate maps of the time, a host of later eighteenth-century navigators tried to make land there, including Lord Anson (1740–44), Commodore Byron (1764), Captain Cook (on his two voyages), Banks and Solander (1769), Pernetty (1763–64) and Bougainville (1769). Only at the end of the century was it officially acknowledged as a phantom island, which almost certainly had been caused by a mistaken sighting of the Falklands to the south.

One of Herman Moll's friends from the coffee shop, the writer and explorer William Dampier, had been on the ship that made the mistaken sighting. Dampier's *A New Voyage Round the World* of 1697 had been a tremendous success that helped inspire the interest in South America and the commercial possibilities of a South Sea company – while ignoring the considerable problem that most of South America was still under Spanish dominion.

It is telling that the illustration to the bottom left of the map should be of Potosí, the silver mine in modern day Bolivia that had brought such indescribable wealth to Spain.

Potosí was one of the richest silver mines ever discovered. Around 1550, not long after their conquest of Peru, the Spanish began extensive mining into Potosí hill, the "*Cerro Rico*" or "Rich Mountain". Indians were brought forcibly from hundreds of miles away to work the mine. A large number of them lost their lives.

The image of the mine as described by contemporary witnesses is Dantesque. The great central shaft of the mine descended into the mountain, with three crude ladders hung from the sides: a "down" ladder, an "up" ladder and a third for use if either of the other two broke, as they frequently did. The Indians would carry enormous loads from the perpetual darkness at the foot of the shaft – one authority quotes 45 kilos, a tremendous weight. As many as 4,500 men could be working in the mine at any one time, with twice that number waiting outside to take their turn.

The mine consumed the labour-force of the South American Altiplano. Within a generation, the population of those parts of the Altiplano used for mine conscription had halved. Within another generation it had halved again. And still Potosí continued to exact its quota.

Any pretence that this was being done voluntarily by the Indians – a pretence that had been sustained at some lesser

mines elsewhere – was washed away by the enormous wealth Potosí created for the Spanish emperor, a wealth which fuelled further misery in Europe with the prosecution of Spain's European wars.

In the elaborate cartouche around the dedication can be seen two volcanoes erupting, possibly a reference to Cotopaxi and Chimborazo in what was then still viceregal Peru (now modern Ecuador). Chimborazo was at that time considered to be the highest mountain in the world.

How enticing it must have been to look at this wonderful map, with the vision of "the Islands of Salomon" in the great South Sea and its illustration of the riches of Potosí and assume that trade to such a distant place could erupt as spectacularly and successfully as a volcano; when in fact it was nothing more than a chimera, and a bubble that would burst.

Guaina Poti, or Yong Potosi

SI lies in the Province of Peru, in Lat. $21\frac{1}{2}$ Deg. S. 'Tis above a Spanish League in Circumference and 1624 Rods high, of the Form of a Sugar loaf, and a sandy Colour. It has four extraordinary rich Veins of Silver Oar, discovered A.D. 1545. They run N. & S. slopingly in y^e East Side of y^e Hill. In 1587 the Rich Vein contain'd 87 Mines, some of wch were above 200 Fathom deep. Here are kept imployd by turns above 20000 Miners. It is generally reported that here are refined annually, for ye King's fifth Part, about 34666 P^d w. of fine Silver, besides what he is deprived of, wch is thought to equal almost the said Sum.

Tarapaia

Left: Potosi. Detail from "Map of South America, According to the Newest and Most Exact Observations", by Herman Moll, *c*.1726. The mine consumed the labour-force of the South American Altiplano.

The Grand Tour

France

For their Grand Tour, British travellers of the eighteenth century needed to negotiate France in order to reach the classical glories of Italy on the other side. They often did so with remarkable ill-humour.

The worst perhaps of all was Tobias Smollett, whose *Travels through France and Italy* of 1766 remains one of the most curmudgeonly travel books ever written. He does not spare the whip when describing the faults of the French, although to be fair, he can be equally damning about the England which he had come from – "the beds paltry, the cookery execrable, the wine poison, the attendance bad, the publicans insolent, and the bills extortionate". The inhabitants of Dover made their living from "smuggling and fleecing strangers".

All this does not put him in a good mood by the time he arrives in Boulogne, having been "tossed about by the sea, cold and weary and languishing for want of sleep". After a difficult landfall, he and his fellow passengers have to walk a mile to the

Below: Illustration from *A Year's Journey through France, and Part of Spain* by Philip Thicknesse, 1778. Thicknesse was a British author, eccentric and friend of the artist Thomas Gainsborough. Like many other British writers, Thicknesse both made the Grand Tour and wrote about it. He travelled with his wife and daughters, a spaniel, a parakeet and a monkey named Jocko, who rode postilion.

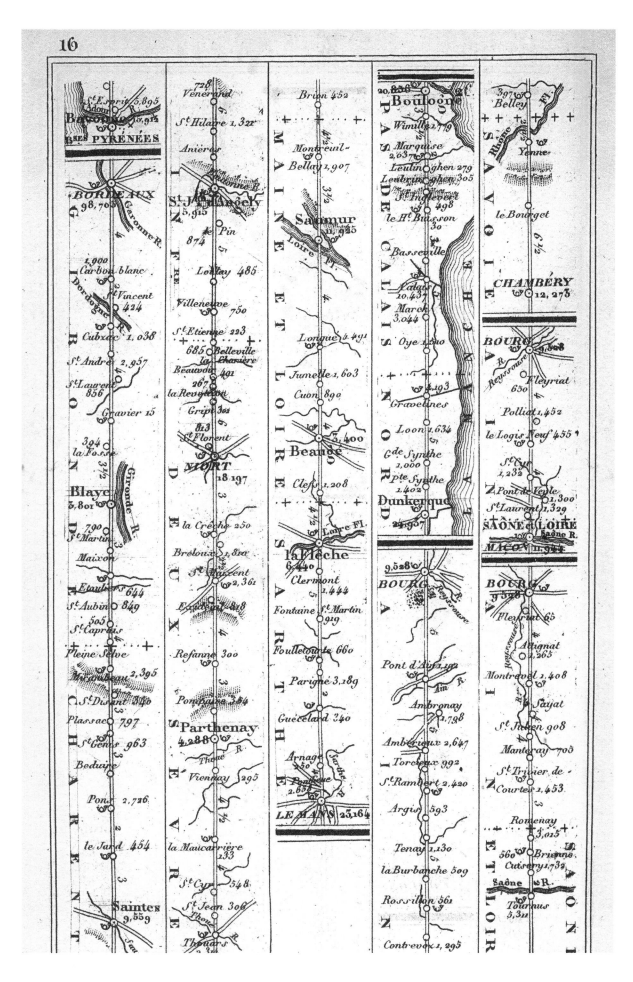

Opposite: Detail from *Nouvel Itineraire Portatif des Principales Routes de France* by Dopter, 1840. This typical strip map was a useful method of showing routes across France in an economical way: a set of short, narrow maps showed just the main road and its side-tunings.

nearest inn, only to find that there are no rooms left so they have to sit up all night in the kitchen.

His rival, Lawrence Sterne – who lampooned Smollett as the dreary, splenetic "Smelfungus" in *A Sentimental Journey through France and Italy*, a bestseller of its day – had a more comfortable time of it and enjoyed his first welcoming dinner of fricasséed chicken. But in general, the English did not find French food to their taste. "I hate French cookery and abominate the garlic," was a typical comment. Charles Burney complained of eating "stale mackerel, salad with rancid oil and an omelette made with raddled eggs". Robert Wharton discovered in 1755, at around the time this traveller's map (opposite) was published, that he had just eaten "no small quantity of fricassee'd frogs ... They tasted exceedingly like veal."

As Smollett made his way across France he was not impressed by its inhabitants. "France is the general reservoir from which all the absurdities of false taste, luxury and extravagance have overflowed to the different kingdoms and states of Europe," he proclaimed. He disliked the way that French women used make-up, as he thought it made them all look the same. He also complained that they had been encouraged from early childhood to say the first thing that ever came into their heads. But in case he was accused of any ungallant prejudice against the fairer sex, he was equally scathing about French men. He felt they were "even more ridiculous and insignificant than the women".

If you were an English lord, you might arrange to hire or buy a carriage to take you across France. But the average traveller – and certainly writer – had to make do with public transport: either using a *carosse*, a stage coach, which could carry six passengers, or the larger *coche*, which could carry 16. Neither was particularly fast, especially if fully laden, and the onward journey to Paris could take a long time.

This meant staying at a great many inns along the road, at which, commented Walter Stanhope in 1769, the beds were "generally occupied with troops of bugs and whole armies of fleas". Moreover, warned Sir Thomas Nugent, who wrote a guidebook for his fellow travellers, "you will not find the beds like ours in England; for they raise them very high, with several thick mattresses: their linen is ill washed and worst dried."

Right: "France, Divided into its Generalities with the Adjacent Coasts of England, Holland, Ireland, Spain, Portugal". By Thomas Jefferys, 1756.

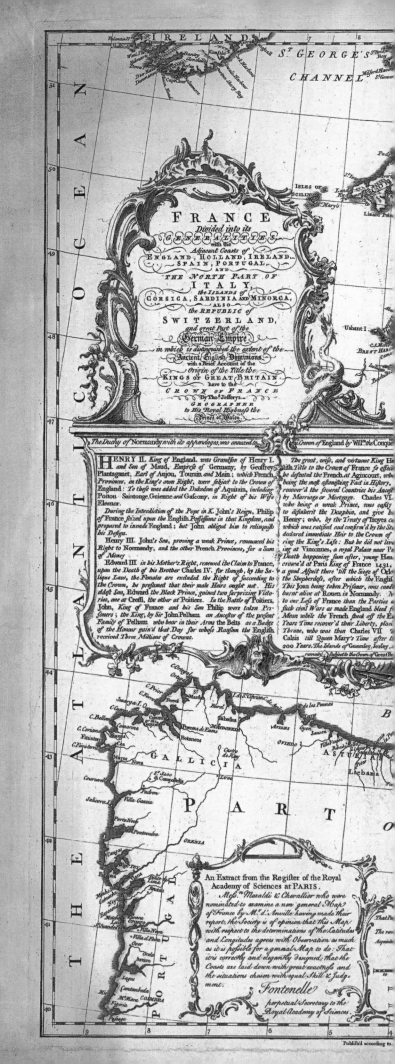

Panel 3 (left):

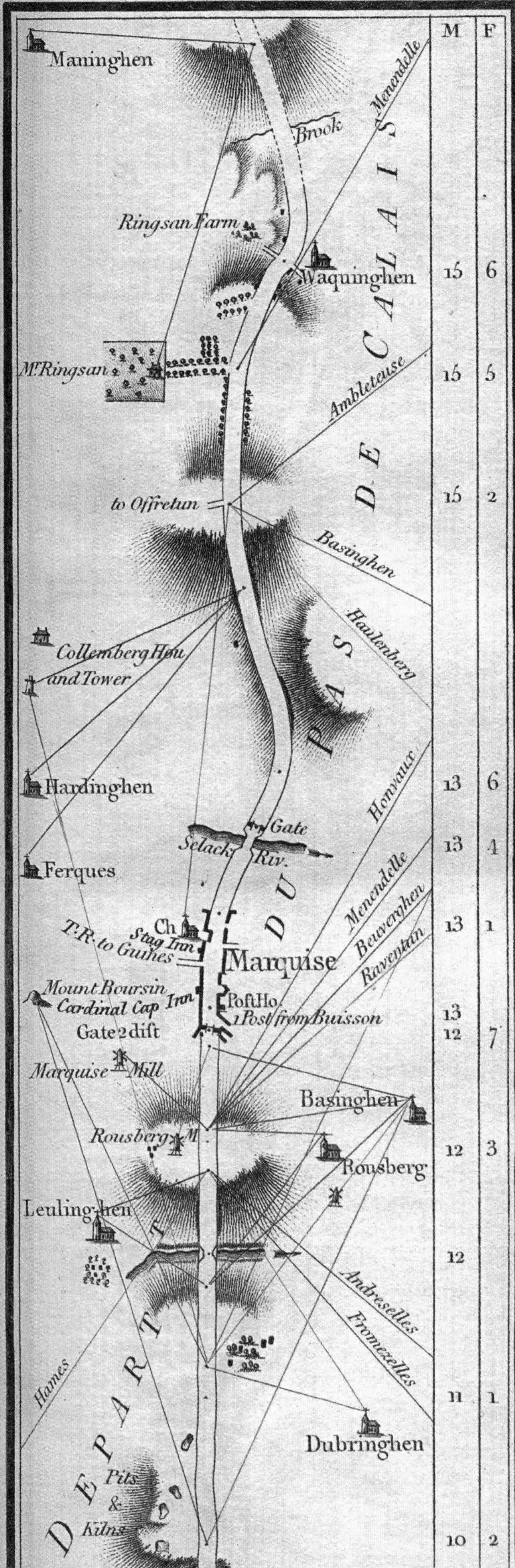

Maninghen

Brook

Menendelle

Ringsan Farm

Waquinghen — M 15 F 6

Ambleteuse

Mr Ringsan — 15 5

to Offretun — 15 2

Basinghen

Hautlenberg

PAS DE CALAIS

Collemberg Hou and Tower

Horvaur

Hardinghen — 13 6

Gate

Selacke Riv. — 13 4

Ferques

Menendelle

Beuverghen

Ravenlin

Ch St ag Inn — 13 1

T.R. to Guihes

Marquise

Mount Boursin Cardinal Cap Inn — 13

Gate 2 dist — Post Ho. 1 Post from Buisson — 12 7

Marquise Mill

Basinghen

Rousberg M — 12 3

Rousberg

Leulinghen

12

Andreselles

Fromexelles

Hames

DEPART

Dubringhen — 11 1

Pits & Kilns — 10 2

DU PAS

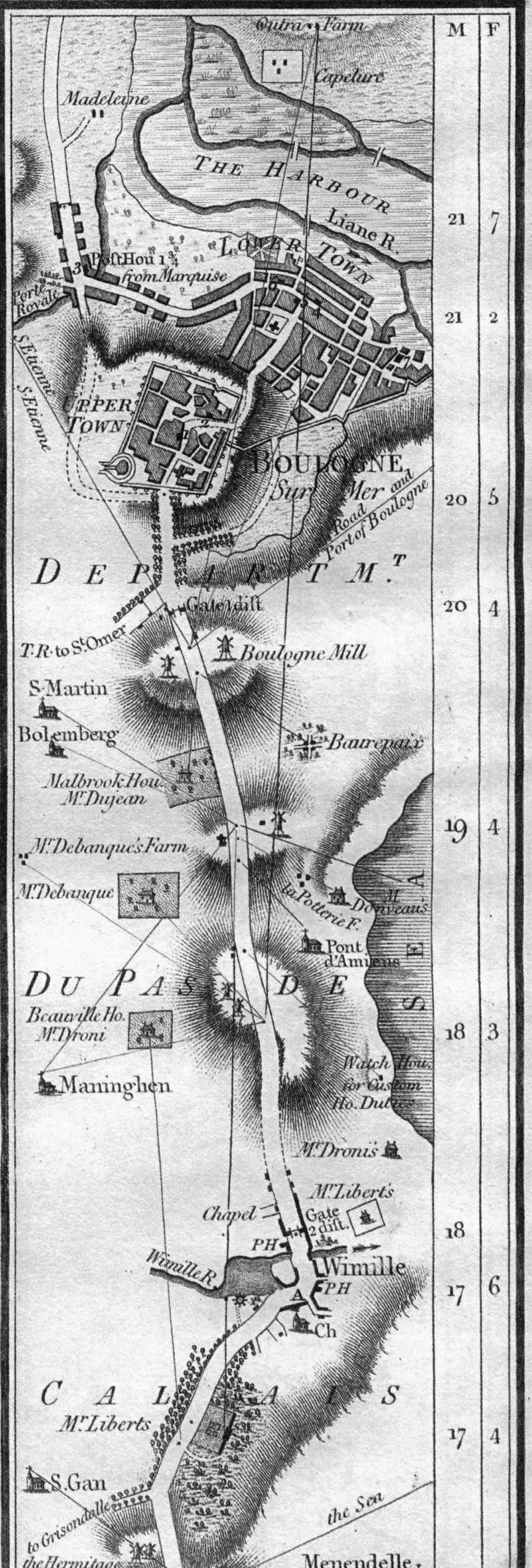

Panel 4 (right):

Outra Farm

Madeleyne

Capelure

THE HARBOUR

Liane R.

LOWER TOWN — M 21 F 7

Port Royale

Post Hou 1¼ from Marquise — 21 2

S. Etienne

UPPER TOWN

BOULOGNE Sur Mer and Road Port of Boulogne — 20 5

DEPARTMᵗ

Gate 2 dist — 20 4

T.R. to St Omer

Boulogne Mill

S. Martin

Bolemberg

Beaurepaix

Malbrook Hou. Mr Dujean

Mr Debanque's Farm — 19 4

Mr Debanque

la Potterie F.

Donvcaus

Pont d'Amiens

DU PAS DE

Beauville Ho. Mr Droni — 18 3

Maninghen

Watch Hou for Custom Ho. Dulies

Mr Dronis

Mr Liberts

Chapel — Gate 2 dist — 18

PH

Wimille R.

PH — Wimille — 17 6

Ch

CALAIS

Mr Liberts — 17 4

S. Gan

to Grisondalle the Hermitage

the Sea

Mr Menville Farm

Menendelle

Beuvreghen — 17

Most British travellers made for Paris and then took a detour so that they could see Versailles before heading further south. However, there was a fashion for decrying the creation of Louis XIV as ambitious but soulless. Lady Mary Wortley Montagu declared that it was "vast, rather than beautiful", Horace Walpole was horrified by the way shopkeepers had set up stalls in the colonnades, while Smollett, as ever, was the most dismissive of all. He pronounced Versailles to be "a dismal habitation".

Those aristocrats doing a full Grand Tour of several years could afford to head down to the Loire Valley for a few months and learn the finer aspects of French riding, wine, food, and dancing, as well as the language itself. Travellers on a tighter

Opposite: Detail from "An Actual Survey and Itinerary of the Road from Calais to Paris" by Louis Hébert and G. Dufont, 1831.

Above: "Cathédrale de Lyon". Illustration from *La France Illustrée*, by V. A. Malte-Brun, 1858.

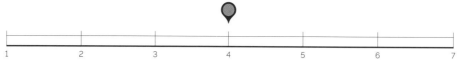

budget would make straight for Lyons, either continuing on the post route or taking a boat down the Saône.

At Lyons and beyond, most British travellers started to get more enthusiastic as they sampled their first "beakers full of the warm South", the wines of Burgundy. The inns were better and cheaper than those in Paris. They could dine on peaches and crayfish, while the inhabitants were thought to be more friendly than in the north of France.

Smollett, as ever, presented a less forgiving view: "Through the whole of the South of France, except in large cities, the inns are cold, damp, dark, dismal and dirty; the landlords equally disobliging and rapacious; the servants awkward, sluttish and slothful." He went on to add, "in general, you are served with the appearance of the most mortifying indifference."

Near Avignon, British travellers could admire the Roman remains at Nîmes and Arles, before proceeding to Montpellier or Toulouse if travelling round the Mediterranean coast – while others chose to make for Geneva and headed over the Alps.

This map shows the sense of entitlement that the British still had for France. It even continues to shade in pink the territory that English Kings once ruled. The rubric alludes to "a brief account of the origin of the title the Kings of Great Britain have to the crown of France". No wonder young British aristocrats should assume the continent was theirs to explore.

Above: "Arles – The Arena, interior". Photographer unknown, 1894.

Opposite: "Arles – The Arena, exterior". Photographer unknown, 1894.

Following pages: "Le Pont du Gard". Illustration from *Histoire des Antiquités de la Ville de Nismes et ses environs*, by Léon Ménard, 1826.

The Grand Tour

Italy

In the course of his travels, a young man generally acquires some knowledge of one or two foreign languages; a knowledge, however, which is seldom sufficient to enable him either to speak or write them with propriety. In other respects he commonly returns home more conceited, more unprincipled, more dissipated, and more incapable of any serious application, either to study or to business, than he could well have become in so short a time had he lived at home.
(Adam Smith, *The Wealth of Nations*, 1776)

The great Scottish economist and writer Adam Smith had a poor opinion of the Grand Tour. When he was Professor of Moral Philosophy at Glasgow University, his lectures were attended by the young James Boswell, who, a few years after this map (pp.46–47) was printed, decided to embark on his own adventures on the continent.

Left: Jean-Jacques Rousseau. On his final return journey to England, Boswell managed to seduce Rousseau's mistress, Thérèse Le Vasseur.

Below: "Vesuvius and surroundings after the eruption of 1631". Engraved by Domenico dell'Acerra after a drawing by Giovanni Morghen.

Opposite: "Carta del Vesuvio compileta per L'Istituto Vulcanologico Immenuel Friedlaender, Napoli". Published by Istituto Geografico Militare, Florence, 1927.

Following pages: "A Map of Italy with its Kingdoms, States &c., from the latest and best observations", 1745.

Whether his mentor Adam Smith would have approved of the results is not recorded, although Smith was amused and attracted by Boswell himself, as were so many of his contemporaries. He praised the young man for his "happy felicity of manners", a phrase Boswell, with characteristic immodesty, hugged to himself for many years.

So in 1763, aged just 23, Boswell set off for Europe, as so many young British men of means would do before and since. But Boswell's was to be no ordinary journey.

Endowed with extraordinary vanity, confidence and some would say presumption, Boswell determined to visit some of the great men of Europe, whether they wanted him to or not. He buttonholed Rousseau and invited himself to dinner with Voltaire.

He also continued with his journals, which for many are some of the finest and most revealing diaries ever written. As a result, we have a full account of his travels and adventures.

He began in Utrecht where he promptly fell in love – not for the first time on this journey – and had to be bustled out of the city when it all went wrong.

CARTA DEL VESUVIO

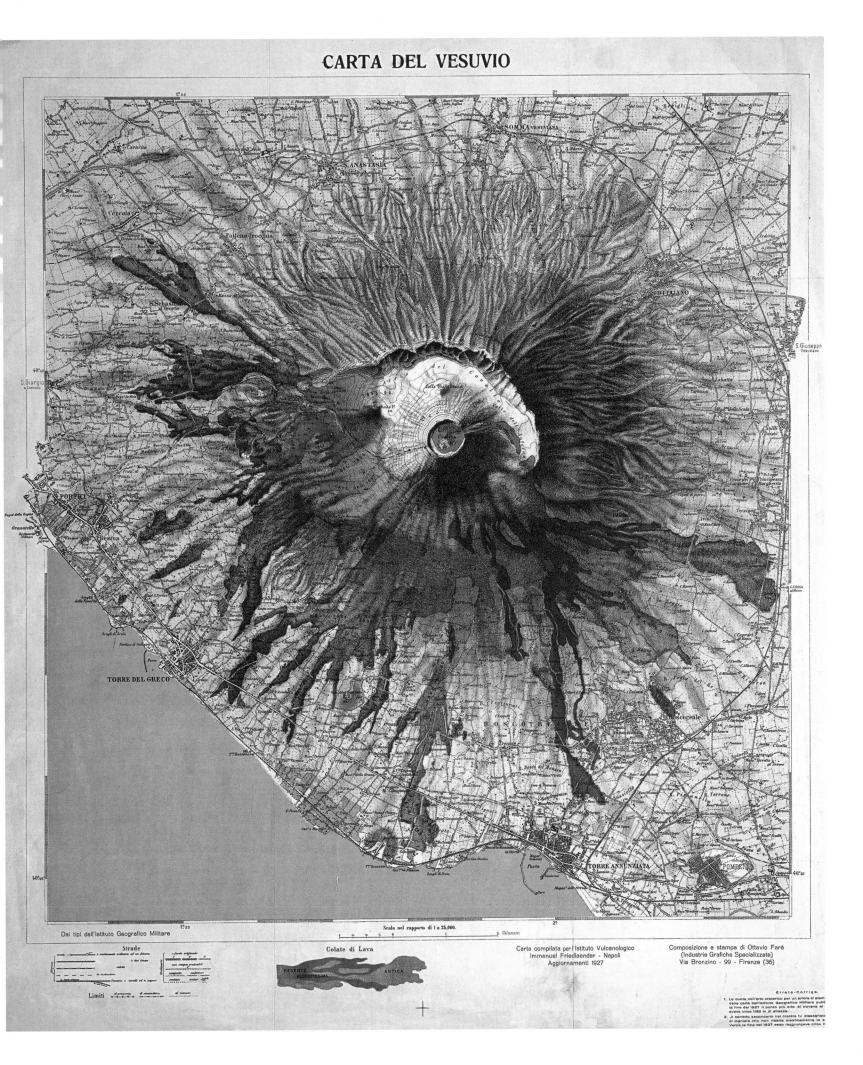

Dai tipi dell'Istituto Geografico Militare

Scala nel rapporto di 1 a 25,000.

Chilometro

Strade

Colate di Lava

RECENTE
RECENTISSIMA   ANTICA

Limiti

Carta compilata per l'Istituto Vulcanologico
Immanuel Friedlaender - Napoli
Aggiornamenti 1927

Composizione e stampa di Ottavio Farè
(Industrie Grafiche Specializzate)
Via Bronzino - 99 - Firenze (36)

Errata-Corrige.

1. Le quote dell'orlo craterico per un errore di stampa della carta dell'Istituto Geografico Militare pubblicata la fine del 1927 il punto più alto si trovava al aveva circa 1180 m di altezza.

2. Il cratere secondario nel cratere fu disegnato di maniera che non risalta plasticamente la Verso la fine del 1927 esso raggiungeva circa 11

EXPLANATION.

⚓ Capital Cities.
‡ Archbishopricks.
† Bishopricks.
⚲ Universities.
⚑ Castles.
P. Principality.
D. Dukedom.
R. Republick.

PART OF SWITZERLAND

THE GRISONS

PART OF TRENT

PART OF DAUPHINE IN FRANCE

PROVENCE

SAVOY

PIEMONT

MILAN

VENICE

PARMA

MODENA

TUSCANY

SEA OF PROVENCE

SEA OF GENOA

SEA OF CORSICA

SEA OF TUSCANY

Straits of Bonifacio

SEA OF SARDINIA

TIRHENIAN SEA

MEDITERRANEAN

A MAP OF ITALY

with its KINGDOMS, STATES &c.

from the latest & best Observations,

*For M*r *Tindal's Continuation of*
*M*r *Rapin's History.*

(1745)

Italian & British Miles, 60 to a Degree.

10 20 30   60   90   120

German Leagues, 15 to a Degree.

5   10   15   20   25   30

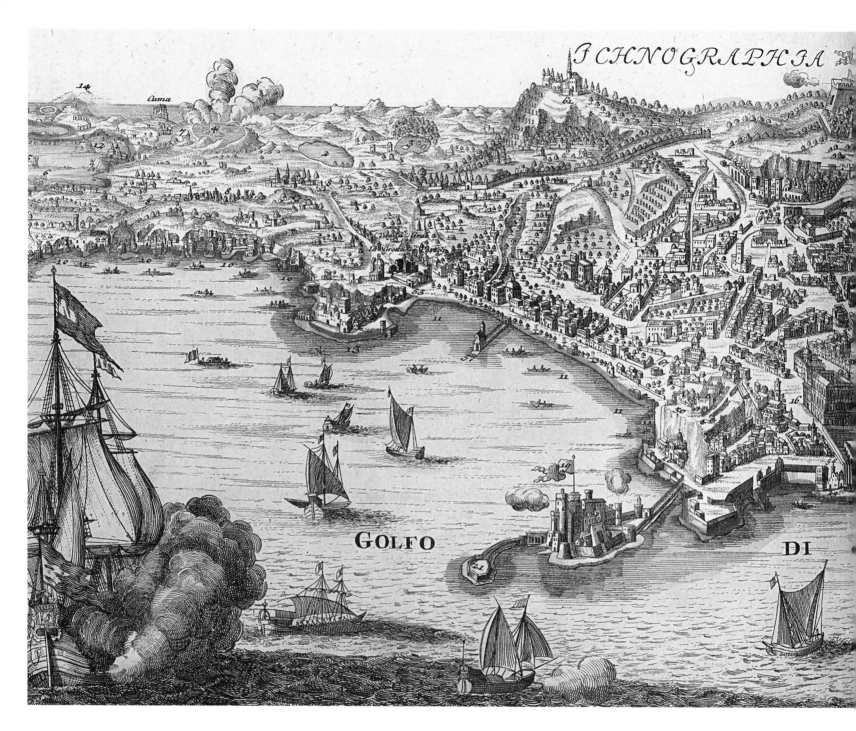

In Turin, Boswell attended a hanging when he saw people rushing past him to the gallows. He jumped out of his chaise and rushed to join them, although he found the spectacle hideous, as the hangmen put his feet on the criminal's head and neck to strangle him when he fell down with the rope. Arriving in Rome, he alternated between seeing great masterpieces like Raphael's *Transfiguration*, chasing pretty women and socializing with émigrés like the radical writer John Wilkes.

He also had his own portrait painted (p.51), by fellow Scot, Gavin Willison. Boswell wore what he describes as his "greatcoat of green camlet lined with fox-skin fur", over a scarlet waistcoat with gold lace – the eighteenth century equivalent of dressing like a rock star.

NEAPOLIS.

NAPOLI.

Willison – who was just beginning his career and was only Boswell's age, 23 – has caught the mixture of searching appraisal in his subject's eyes and the sensuous disposition of his mouth and full lips.

It then took Boswell "five disagreeable days" to reach Naples along the Appian Way, but the journey was worth it. During his three-week stay he visited the Royal Palace at Portacini, climbed

Vesuvius and was given a personal tour through Pompeii and Herculaneum by Camillo Paderni, the Italian painter curating the antiquities.

Above: The Bay of Naples. Detail of a plate from *Atlas Novus Terrarum Orbis Imperia, Regna et Status Exactis Tabulis Geographicè Demonstrans*, 1730, by Johann Baptist Homann.

AN
ACCOUNT
OF
CORSICA,
THE JOURNAL OF A TOUR
TO THAT ISLAND;
AND MEMOIRS OF
PASCAL PAOLI.

BY JAMES BOSWELL, Esq;

ILLUSTRATED with a New and Accurate MAP of CORSICA.

Non enim propter gloriam, divitias aut honores pugnamus, sed propter liber-
tatem solummodo, quam nemo bonus nisi simul cum vita amittit.
Lit. Comit. et Baron. Scotiae ad Pap. A. D. 1320.

GLASGOW,

PRINTED BY ROBERT AND ANDREW FOULIS FOR
EDWARD AND CHARLES DILLY IN THE POULTRY, LONDON
MDCCLXVIII.

In a letter to a friend, he eulogized the classical scene, "where the finest of bays is diversified by islands and bordered by fields where Virgil's Muses charmed the Creation".

He also "ran after girls without restraint. My blood was inflamed by the burning climate, and my passions were violent. I indulged them; my mind had almost nothing to do with it." He justified this by citing "the rakish deeds of Horace and other amorous Roman poets". It would be unwise to assume that young British aristocrats went on the Grand Tour just to improve their minds.

After further amorous and cultural adventures in both Venice and Siena, Boswell found himself in Corsica. His earlier encounter with Rousseau had interested him in the independence movement taking place on the island, led by Pasquale di Paoli, and he joined the rebels with romantic enthusiasm, even dressing up in a Corsican costume with pistols.

There was an old witticism in eighteenth-century circles that there was only one reason why an Englishman should ever want to go to France: to get to Italy on the other side. Boswell, although of course Scottish, followed suit, and spent as little time in France as he could both on his outward and return journey. He found the food and inns of poor quality, the carriages very slow and the French themselves "impudent". He already regretted leaving Italy. "Oh Italy! Land of felicity! True seat of all elegant delight!" he exclaimed.

On his final return journey to England, Boswell managed to seduce Rousseau's mistress, Thérèse Le Vasseur, whom he had persuaded to accompany him to London. Any feeling of triumph at having thus associated with the great man himself in such an intimate way was soon dashed when Thérèse – who, aged 43, was some 20 years Boswell's senior – complained that he had "no art to his lovemaking". Seeing the young Boswell look downcast at this, she added, "I did not mean to hurt you. You are young, you can learn. I myself will give you your first lesson in the art of love."

So finished Boswell's remarkable two-year tour of the continent. The unusually candid journals he kept were not discovered until the twentieth century, and so were only

published then – perhaps luckily, as an earlier age might have censored them.

What was published then, and so was accessible to young aristocrats, was this fine copper-engraved map of Italy. As the title in the top right notes, in a typically decorative cartouche ornamented with scrolls and flowers, it was prepared for a new edition of Paul Rapin's *History of England*, a staple of every eighteenth-century gentleman's library, not least because over 10 elaborate volumes it promoted the Hanoverian view of history and therefore the legitimacy of the Georgian reign.

Opposite: Title page from *An Account of Corsica, the Journal of a Tour to that Island ...* by James Boswell, 1768. Boswell joined the rebels with romantic enthusiasm, even dressing up in a Corsican costume with pistols.

Above: Boswell was endowed with extraordinary vanity, confidence and some would say presumption.

The Grand Tour

Rome

For most English aristocrats making the Grand Tour, the climax and culmination of it all was Rome. This 1780 map of "Ancient Rome" (pp.54–55) shows what awaited them.

We have many travellers' accounts of the time, which show that along with the classical wonders of the old imperial city – "one cannot walk 50 paces without observing some remains of its ancient grandeur," said one visitor – came considerable frustration.

On arriving in the city, customs house officials would take it upon themselves, particularly if the carriage was of an English "milord", to make a savage and thorough search for potential contraband goods, which would only cease on the offering of a propitious bribe. Then a mob of *servitori di piazza* "would offer their services with the most disagreeable importunity", sometimes climbing uninvited into carriages with the presumption of locals who felt entitled to appoint themselves as guides.

The French writer Charles de Brosses noted sardonically that a quarter of the population of Rome were priests, a quarter statues and a quarter people who did nothing. The rest were visitors, many of them, he noted, English and often very rich.

Horace Walpole had a low opinion of his fellow English tourists, who he thought "either schoolboys just broke loose or old fools that have come abroad at 40 to see the world", while Lady Mary Wortley Montagu was equally appalled by the bossy and pedantic tutors who accompanied their charges.

The artist Thomas Jones, arriving in Rome in 1776, was not impressed by the state of the accommodation:

My curtain-less bed consisted of a large bag of straw and mattress, placed on a few boards, which were supported by two iron benches. In this melancholy chamber, or rather chapel, I retired to rest, and lulled to sleep by the pattering of the rain against the windows, sometimes dreamed of the many enjoyments I had left behind me in London.

Tempio di Quirino

Casa di Flauio Sabino

Casa di Pomponio Attico

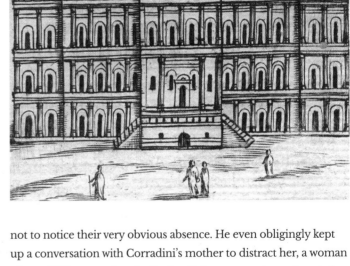

PALAZZO MAGGIORE

The area around Piazza di Spagna had so many English visitors that it became known as "the English ghetto". Thomas Jones visited a coffee house there, which he found "a filthy, vaulted room, the walls of which were painted with sphinxes, obelisks and pyramids, from capricious designs of Piranesi ..."

But despite these inconveniences and the occasional squalor, there was much to delight the visitor, particularly if he could find a reliable guide who knew what he was doing. One such was the celebrated Johann Winckelmann, who at the time this map was printed was the Chief Supervisor of Antiquities in Rome.

It was Winckelmann who guided the English radical writer John Wilkes around Rome and impressed him both by his deep knowledge and by his discreet tact. When Wilkes wanted to disappear for a few moments with his mistress, Gertrude Corradini, to make love behind a convenient ruin, Winckelmann pretended

not to notice their very obvious absence. He even obligingly kept up a conversation with Corradini's mother to distract her, a woman who, as Wilkes noted tartly, "had as little conversation as beauty".

The classical ruins were often used and abused with similar familiarity by the inhabitants. The Palatine was covered in weeds and contained "a few tattered robe makers working in the

Opposite: "Porta Maggiore e condotto dell'Acqua Claudia". Illustration from *Descrizione di Roma Antica*, 1697.

Above, left: "Della Casa di Pomponio Attico, di quella di Flavio Sabino, e del Tempio di Quirino". Illustration from *Descrizione di Roma Antica*, 1697.

Above, right: "Del Palazzo di Augusto, ouero Maggiore". Illustration from *Descrizione di Roma Antica*, 1697.

Following pages: "Roma ... Administro Urbis Ichnographiam ..." by Bufalino and Nolli, 1748, re-engraved by Brun, *c.*1780.

shade"; the Arch of Septimus Severus sheltered a barbershop; a grocery market was held in the Forum twice a week; while James Boswell noted with his usual candour that animals were allowed to graze all over the Colosseum and so "several portions were full of dung".

The Colosseum of course loomed large over the imaginations of all those travellers who arrived in Rome. It was Vespasian who had originally presented the people of Rome with this ambitious stadium, which had the advantage of being far more centrally located than previous arenas.

One reason the Colosseum was both ambitious and innovative was that it was free-standing; most such amphitheatre were built into a slope so that at least one side was naturally supported. It was also huge, although that is not, contrary to what might be supposed, why it was called the Colosseum; the name comes from a giant statue of Nero that was all that survived from his *Domus Aurus* (Golden House) complex. Vespasian replaced his offending head with that of Apollo (an incongruous transplant), but the bronze statue continued on the same site well into the medieval ages and was as much a symbol of the city as the Colosseum.

That said, the Colosseum was of course massive: over 150 feet high, ringed by a wall almost a third of a mile long and enclosing over five acres, with 300 tons of iron clamps needed just to hold

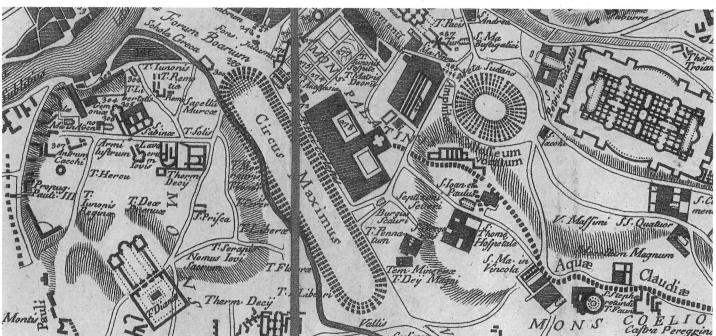

Opposite, above: The celebrated Johann Winckelmann, who at the time this map (pp. 54–55) was printed was the Chief Supervisor of Antiquities in Rome.

Opposite, below: The Circus Maximus, detail from "Roma … Administro Urbis Ichnographiam …" by Bufalino and Nolli, 1748, re-engraved by Brun, c.1780.

Above: "Dell' Anfiteatro di Vespasiano, chiamato Colosseo, e sua descrizzione". Illustration from *Descrizione di Roma Antica*, 1697. James Boswell noted with his usual candour that animals were allowed to graze all over the Colosseum and so "several portions were full of dung".

Horti di Salustio

Campo Scelerato

Above: "De' Giardini di Salustio; e del Campo Scelerato".
Illustration from *Descrizione di Roma Antica*, 1697.

Opposite: Detail of "Roma … Administro Urbis Ichnographiam …"
by Bufalino and Nolli, 1748, re-engraved by Brun, *c.*1780.

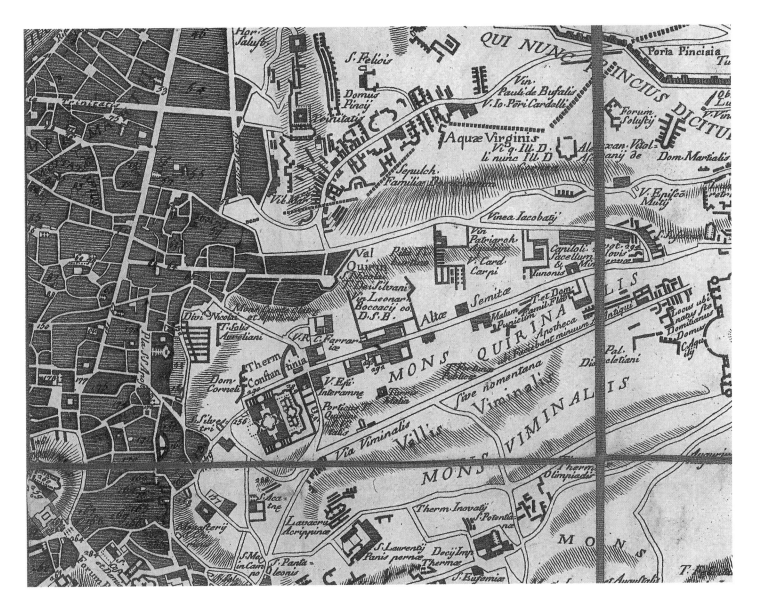

its stones together. It was made up of both an outer wall (already largely fallen by the eighteenth century) and an inner wall which has been far better preserved. A "wedding cake" effect was achieved by having a far taller attic layer in which women and slaves sat, being ranked equally by the Romans, above the three more regular arcades below.

Perhaps the most significant visitor to Rome at the time of this map was Edward Gibbon, the historian. One evening in October 1764, he climbed up the hill of the Capitol. Looking out over the Colosseum and the other ruins of Imperial Rome, and with the sound of barefooted friars singing litanies in the church of Santa Maria d'Aracoeli, he "conceived the

first thought" of what was to become *The Decline and Fall of the Roman Empire*, perhaps the greatest historical elegy ever written. Then he marked out the ruins of the Forum, noting "each memorable spot where Romulus stood, Kylie spoke, or Caesar fell".

Gibbon's "cool and minute investigation" of the city was a model of all that the Grand Tour could provide. While there were many rich and foolish aristocrats who brought back nothing but fake "masterpieces" and gonorrhoea from their European adventures, there were also some, like Gibbon and Lord Burlington, with his Palladian inspiration for the country houses of England, who returned genuinely inspired.

The End of the Grand Tour

Byron in the Mediterranean

When this map (pp.62–63) was published in 1804, much had changed since the glory days of the eighteenth century Grand Tour. Europe was at war. In that same year, Napoleon had proclaimed himself Emperor. The illustrations in the map tend not to be scenic spots, but of rocky capes like Finisterre and St Vincent which the British Navy now found itself constantly patrolling.

So when Lord Byron set off on his poetical travels, which he memorialized first in *Childe Harold* – a great sensation and success when it was published – and then in his more scandalous masterpiece, *Don Juan*, he was catering to an armchair public back in Britain who could now only enjoy the pleasures of the Mediterranean vicariously.

Byron certainly set out to enjoy it himself when he set sail on the Lisbon packet from Falmouth on 2 July 1809, "frolicsome as a kitten". Since Italy was as out of bounds as France – aside from Sicily, it was completely controlled by Napoleon or his satraps – the young 21-year-old poet would have to make do with Portugal and Spain.

He was certainly only too keen to leave Britain for a variety of reasons, which included his emotional entanglements with both women and men. Over the next 15 years before his death in Greece in 1824, he spent no less than 11 of them abroad around the Mediterranean.

His voyage to Lisbon took four and a half days, which at the time was considered excellent going. He was less impressed by Lisbon than by nearby Sintra, which he immediately proclaimed to be "perhaps the most beautiful city in the world". As it was one of the first cities he had seen outside England, this may have been premature.

Above: Lord Byron.

Opposite, above: "Picnic outside Constantinople". Watercolour by William Purser, 1790–1852.

Opposite, below: "The Towers, opposite Kandili in Constantinople". Watercolour by William Purser, 1790–1852

Indeed, as soon as he got to Seville in Spain, he found that city delighted him even more; perhaps persuaded by the women whom he described as having "long black hair, dark languishing eyes, clear olive complexions, and forms more graceful in motion than can be conceived by an Englishman used to the drowsy, listless air of his countrywomen." This was the description he gave to his mother; to his friends, he commented on how free and easy were the married women with their charms.

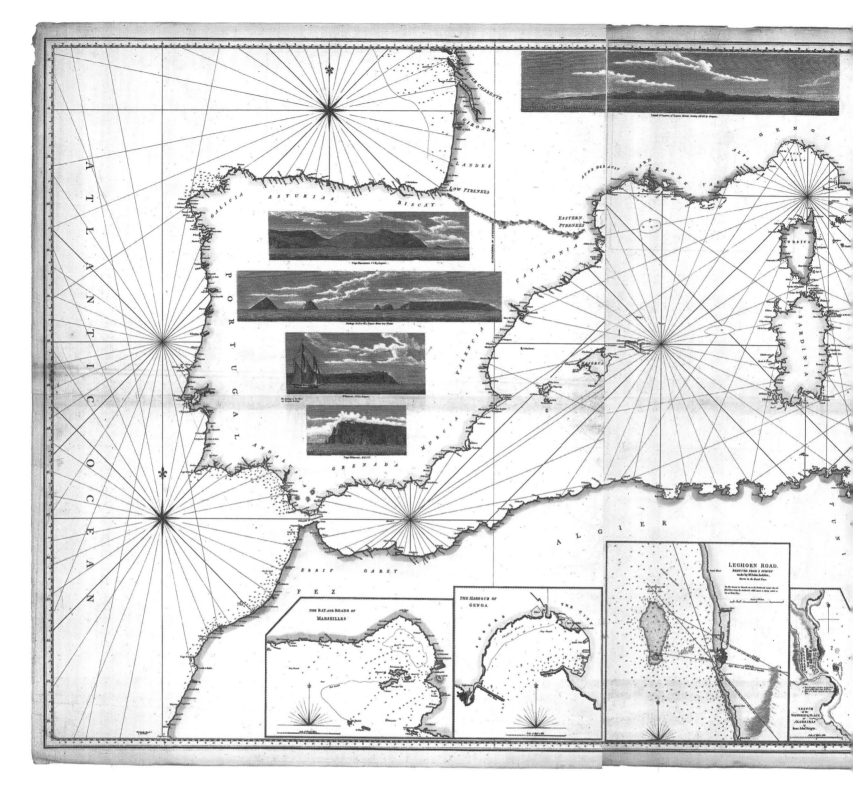

He was less taken by Gibraltar, which he described as "the dirtiest, most detestable spot in existence", and soon sailed for Malta, which he was able to do because as this map indicates – it was drawn up from advice given by a rear admiral of the fleet – the British Navy still controlled the sea, if not the mainland.

Byron was not travelling lightly. Together with his friend Hobhouse, he had four leather trunks, each weighing about 80 pounds, and several smaller ones; three complete beds,

together with all the bedding; and some English saddles, in case foreign ones were too uncomfortable.

They soon had an opportunity to test the saddles. Landing in Albania, which was under the control of the Ottoman Empire, they travelled inland to visit the ruler, Ali Pasha. Byron was much taken by the romance of Albania and compared it to that of his mother's native Scotland: "I was struck forcibly by their resemblance to the Highlanders …

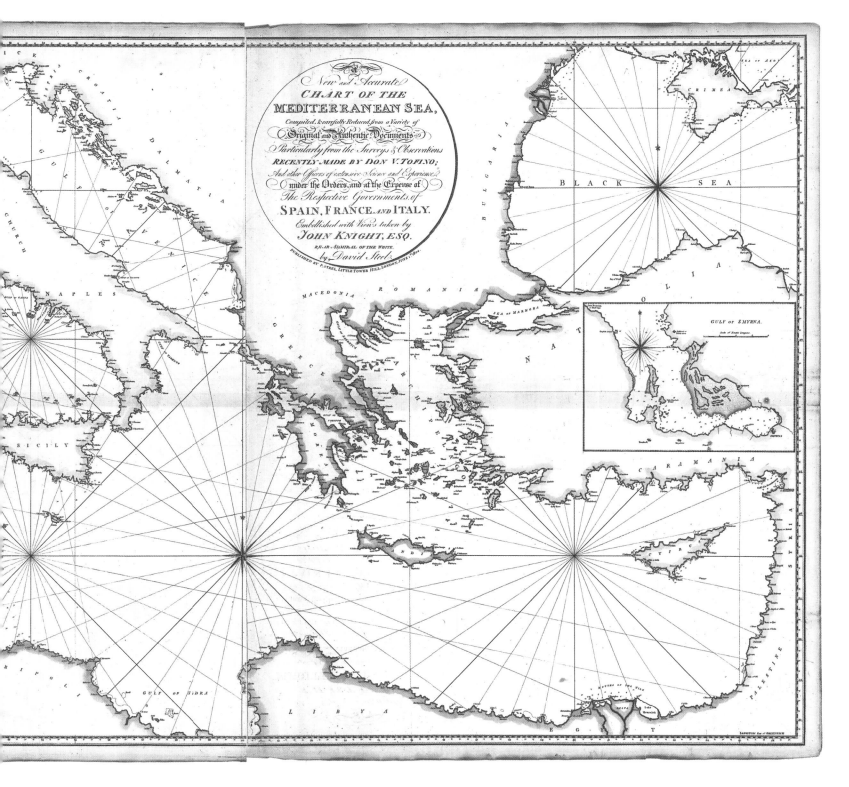

Their very mountains seemed Caledonian, with a kinder climate." He made his first visit to Missolonghi in Greece, to which he was to return many years later when he fought for the cause of Greek independence.

He reached Athens on Christmas day of 1809 and was delighted by the view – "a glorious prospect" – but appalled at what Lord Elgin had done recently in removing the marbles from the Parthenon: "this robbery of ruins from Athens, to instruct the English in sculpture (who are as capable of sculpture as the Egyptians are of skating)".

It is often said that Byron had the mind of a classicist and the heart of a romantic. The antithetical nature of his personality inspired some of his best work. How typical that when he visited

Above: "A New and Accurate Chart of the Mediterranean Sea, Compiled & carefully Reduced from a Variety of Original and Authentic Documents ..." by David Steel, 1804. Embellished with views taken by John Knight, Esq.

CULTURAL TRAVEL 1680–1810

the great Temple to Poseidon on Cape Sounion – still one of Greece's most inspiring ruins – he should carve his name on one of the columns.

After Greece he visited Smyrna (modern Izmir) and the plains of Troy, where he imagined himself wandering over barrows containing the bodies of Achilles, Ajax and other heroes. And then to Constantinople, where, on 3 May, 1810, he swam across the Hellespont, no mean achievement for a man with a club foot and one to which he constantly referred in later life. The crossing had been made famous in classical times by Ovid who claimed that Leander had swum it nightly to see his mistress, Hero; although Byron adds with characteristic sardonicism that Leander's conjugal powers must always have been exhausted by the swim.

This first journey across the Mediterranean transformed Byron. It was not just a pleasure trip. He came to define himself as someone who lived in "the clime of the East" as opposed to what he saw as the hidebound hypocrisy of England.

For the rest of his life he would return to what he had made an alternative homeland. By 1816, when he had become one of the most notorious figures in Britain, he was only too ready to escape his creditors, his wife and English society. After the fall

of Napoleon, he was now able to travel overland to Geneva, where he could meet Percy and Mary Shelley for the famous house party that produced *Frankenstein*; and then travel on to Italy where he pursued both women and classical ruins with some gusto. But Greece continued to lure him.

He returned there via Ithaca, when he could inspect the ruins associated with Homer and Odysseus, and joined the Greek independence movement, only to die of a fever in April 1824. His last letter to his Italian mistress and great love, Teresa Guiccioli, told her that "the Spring is come – I have seen a swallow today – and it was time."

Above: "Hellespont or ye Straits of Constantinople. By Capt. Bamburg" and "The Gulf of Smirna". Details from "Map of Asia..." by Herman Moll, c.1726. Byron famously swam across the Hellespont, no mean achievement for a man with a club foot.

Opposite, above: "Trojan buildings on the north side, and in the great trench cut through the whole hill". Plate from *Troy and its Remains; A Narrative of Researches and Discoveries Made on the Site of Ilium, and in the Trojan Plain*, by Dr Henry Schliemann, 1875. The plains of Troy, where Byron imagined himself wandering over barrows containing the bodies of Achilles, Ajax and other heroes.

Opposite, below: "View of Hissarlik from the north. After the Excavations". Plate from *Troy and its Remains; A Narrative of Researches and Discoveries Made on the Site of Ilium, and in the Trojan Plain*, by Dr Henry Schliemann, 1875.

Following pages: "Constantinople". Watercolour by Joseph Brown, 1850.

II

Adventurous Travel

1810–1900

Right: "Bartholomew's Tourist's Map of Egypt and the Lower Nile, prepared from the latest surveys", 1897.

Select Views of the Lake District

I know not how to give the reader a distinct image of this, the main demarcation of the country, more readily than by requesting him to place himself with me, in imagination, upon some given point; let it be the top of either of the mountains, Great Gavel, or Scawfell; or, rather, let us suppose our station to be a cloud hanging midway between those two mountains, at not more than half a mile's distance from the summit of each, and but a few yards above their highest elevation, he will then see stretched at his feet a number of Vallies, not fewer than nine, diverging from the point, on which he is supposed to stand, like spokes from the nave of a wheel.

(William Wordsworth, *Select Views in Cumberland, Westmoreland, and Lancashire*, 1810)

How Wordsworth came to write a guide to the Lake District is both fascinating and revealing. For many years he refused to do so, on the grounds that he wrote poetry, not prose and that, as he said in a letter of 1808 after ten years living in the Lakes, he now knew them too well "to know where to begin, and where to end".

But only a year or so later he changed his mind, partly out of financial necessity – his poems weren't selling – and because an opportunity fell into his lap. A painter called Joseph Wilkinson had been a neighbour of the Wordsworths before moving to Norfolk. The flat landscape made him nostalgic for the Lakes, so he embarked on a book of *Select Views in Cumberland, Westmoreland, and Lancashire*. He asked Wordsworth to write the accompanying text.

As the art-book was being sold by subscription at a hefty price – £6 6s, so over £200 today in real terms – this was a good commission. When it came out in 1810, the publishers declared the paper "so luxuriously thick, it would admit of tinting" should subscribers want to add their own colour to the engravings.

An unexpected commission can be liberating for a writer; to lay aside the imaginative necessity – or burden – of creating your own work *ex nihilo*, and instead craft to order.

Wordsworth may have been liberated by knowing that what he was doing would be accompanied by illustrations. Or rather, the illustrations, which were very much the main event, were accompanied by his text. When the book was advertised, it hardly mentioned his name. So the words didn't have to work so hard.

Necessity forced Wordsworth to find a way of writing about the Lakes. And his way of doing so was what today we might call psychogeographical: by dividing the district into a wheel, with each valley representing one of the spokes, giving unity but also variety, he could isolate the tone and character of each valley, and suffuse them with personal experience. As a contemporary critic put it in *The Monthly Review*, the strategy was "as topographically useful as it is poetically picturesque".

Moreover, Wordsworth tried to address the Lake District as a holistic experience. Previous guides – of which there had been

Above: "A Map of the Country in the Vicinity of the Lakes". From *A Guide to the Lakes in Cumberland, Westmorland and Lancashire, with Twenty Views of Local Scenery, and a Travelling Map of the Adjacent Country* by John D. D. Robinson, 1819.

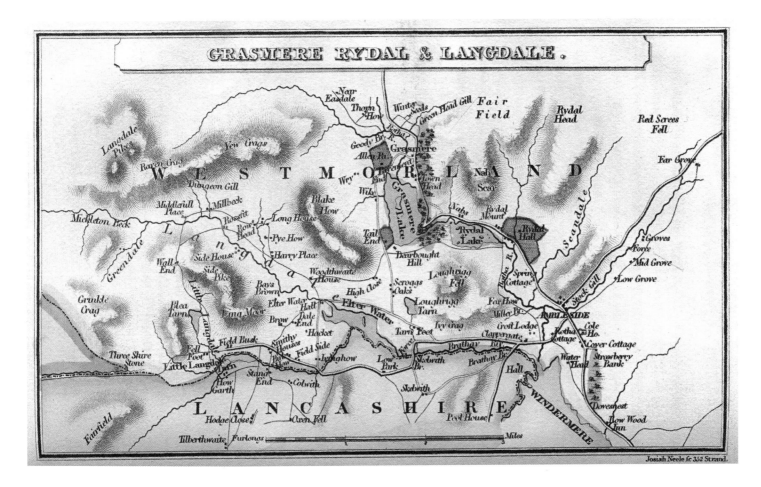

GRASMERE RYDAL & LANGDALE.

many in the eighteenth century – broke the Lakes down into a series of views, rather like a modern tour where you only get off the coach for designated moments. They even recommended travelling with a special viewing instrument, called a Claude Glass, a convex fold-up mirror. Named after Claude Lorrain, whose paintings of Arcadia had done so much to shape British theories of the picturesque, these devices framed and tinted the landscape. To use one, the viewer had to turn their backs to the natural scene and hold up the mirror – much like a modern tourist taking a selfie.

Wordsworth provided the interstices: the people and incidental detail along the way that could make the journey a more lived experience. Although that didn't stop him, like any good poet, from getting bored at writing so much prose. Close to the end, his sister Dorothy recorded that he persuaded her to "compose a description or two for the finishing of his work for Wilkinson", as he had started to find it "irksome". And there is a fine bohemian swagger to the way he disdains the "humble and tedious task" of providing any directions; and the way, familiar

to today's sensitive travel writers, that he resists all attempts to call his "a guidebook".

Nor is he above a little helpful cross-promotion. When moved to quote verse by the sublime quality of any scene, the poetry he most often remembers is invariably his own.

Only in 1822 did Wordsworth finally issue the guide as a standalone volume: *A Description of the Scenery of the Lakes in the North of England*, with a map that folded out and a new section of "Directions and Information for the Tourist". Dorothy added an account of climbing Scafell, then the most tantalizing of lake peaks for the visitor, being remote and not easy to summit. The many editions that followed were a steady earner throughout Wordsworth's long life. Given that he had done so much to

Opposite: "Buttermere Lake and Honister Crag". Early hand–coloured lantern slide, photographer unknown, c.1880–1900.

Above: "Grasmere, Rydal & Langdale". From *Leigh's Guide to the Lakes and Mountains of Cumberland*, 1835. This was the part of the Lake District that Wordsworth knew best.

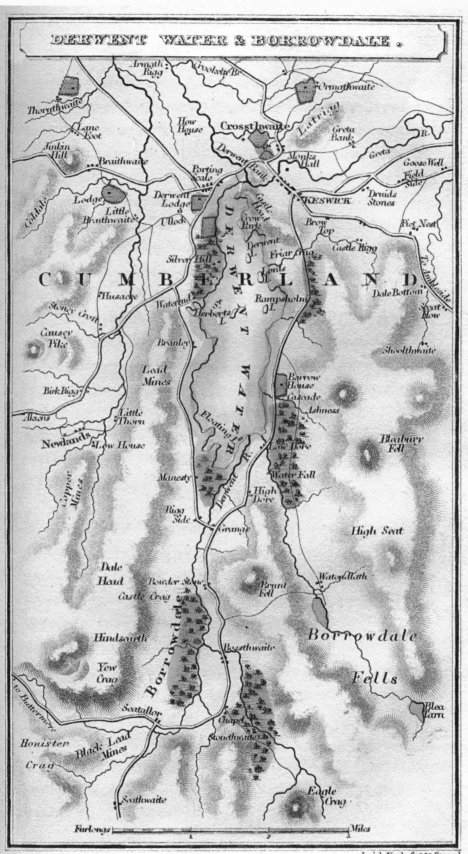

DERWENT WATER & BORROWDALE.

Josiah Neele sc 352 Strand.

attract tourists to the Lake District in the first place, it seemed only fair he should profit from them.

Wordsworth may have been influenced throughout this process by the success of a guidebook about the Lake District by a clergyman called Thomas West, first published in 1778. This led to so many other illustrated guides being produced that one commentator has described them as being the "photographic calendars" of the age.

In 1819 a rector in Westmorland called John Robinson produced yet another, called *A Guide to the Lakes in Cumberland, Westmorland, and Lancashire* and issued it with the fine foldout map that is illustrated on p.71. It is noticeable how even now, when they had become such points of interest, so few of the actual mountains are identified: neither Helvellyn nor Scafell

Pike get a mention. But Wordsworth himself might have been mollified at the appearance of this competitor – for Robinson tactfully quotes from no less than 10 passages of Wordsworth, including *The Excursion*. Seldom has a poet or writer managed to make a part of the world so exclusively their own.

Opposite: "Derwent Water & Borrowdale". From *Leigh's Guide to the Lakes and Mountains of Cumberland, Westmorland and Lancashire*, 1835. So many illustrated guides to the Lakes were being produced that one commentator has described them as being the "photographic calendars" of the age.

Below: "A Map of the Country in the Vicinity of the Lakes", detail. From *A Guide to the Lakes in Cumberland, Westmorland and Lancashire, with Twenty Views of Local Scenery, and a Travelling Map of the Adjacent Country* by John D. D. Robinson, 1819.

Following pages: "Grasmere". Illustration from *A Guide to the Lakes in Cumberland, Westmorland and Lancashire*, 1789. The Lakes were often broken down into a series of views, rather like a modern tour where you only get off the coach for designated moments.

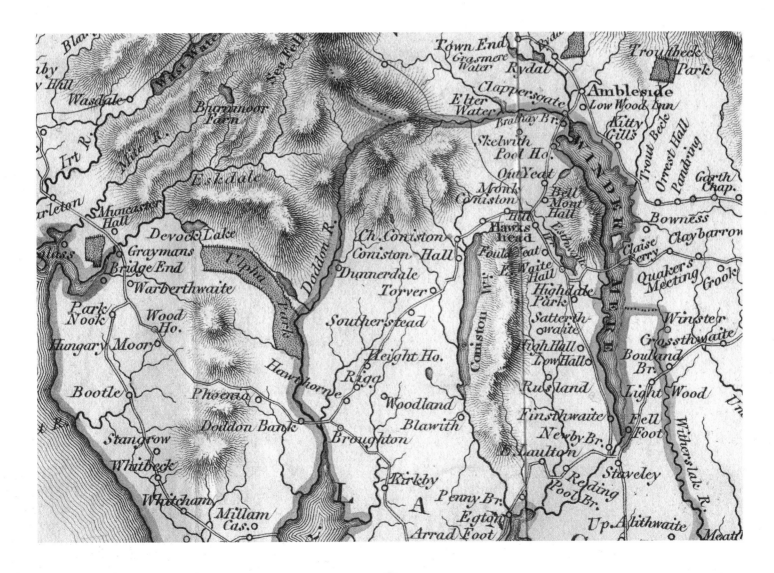

Where the Pyramids Still Stand

When we reached the pier we found an army of Egyptian boys with donkeys no larger than themselves, waiting for passengers—for donkeys are the omnibuses of Egypt. We preferred to walk, but we could not have our own way. The boys crowded about us, clamoured around us, and slewed their donkeys exactly across our path, no matter which way we turned. They were good-natured rascals, and so were the donkeys. We mounted, and the boys ran behind us and kept the donkeys in a furious gallop ... I believe I would rather ride a donkey than any beast in the world.

(*The Innocents Abroad*, Mark Twain, 1869)

Mark Twain was just one of many American and European tourists who gravitated to Egypt in the nineteenth century; he was, however, unusual in that he left a characteristically sharp-eyed and pungent description of his experiences. On collecting one of the aforementioned donkeys, he found himself on a charge through the streets of Cairo,

> *... as nobody can steer a donkey, and some collided with camels, dervishes, effendis, asses, beggars and everything else that offered to the donkeys a reasonable chance for a collision. When we turned into the broad avenue that leads out of the city toward Old Cairo, there was plenty of room. The walls of stately date-palms that fenced the gardens and bordered the way, threw their shadows down and made the air cool and bracing. We rose to the spirit of the time and the race became a wild rout, a stampede, a terrific panic. I wish to live to enjoy it again.*

Twain arrived in Egypt in 1867 aboard the steamship *Quaker City*, as part of a much longer journey he was making right around Europe and the Middle East. A San Francisco newspaper had sponsored his "Great Pleasure Excursion" by commissioning a series of articles, later published as *The Innocents Abroad* (1869).

On arriving at the Pyramids, Twain was horrified to see a fellow tourist clambering up the Sphinx with a hammer to knock off a chunk as a souvenir; but equally pleased when he realized "the Egyptian granite which has defied the storms and earthquakes of all time has nothing to fear from the tack hammers of ignorant excursionists – highwaymen – like this specimen".

The Sphinx itself left a memorable impression on him. He described it as being as large as New York's Fifth Avenue Hotel, and carved out of one single solid block of stone.

Opposite: "Cairo, a saddle donkey". Photograph by Messrs. G. Lekegian & Co., *c*.1890. "I believe I would rather ride a donkey than any beast in the world." – Mark Twain when in Egypt.

Below: "Side view of the Great Sphinx". Plate from *Egypt and Nubia from drawings made on the spot* by David Roberts, RA, 1846–49.

Following pages: "Bartholomew's Tourist's Map of Egypt and the Lower Nile, prepared from the latest surveys", 1897

The Great Sphinx, Pyramids of Gizeh.

David Roberts R.A. L.Haghe lith.

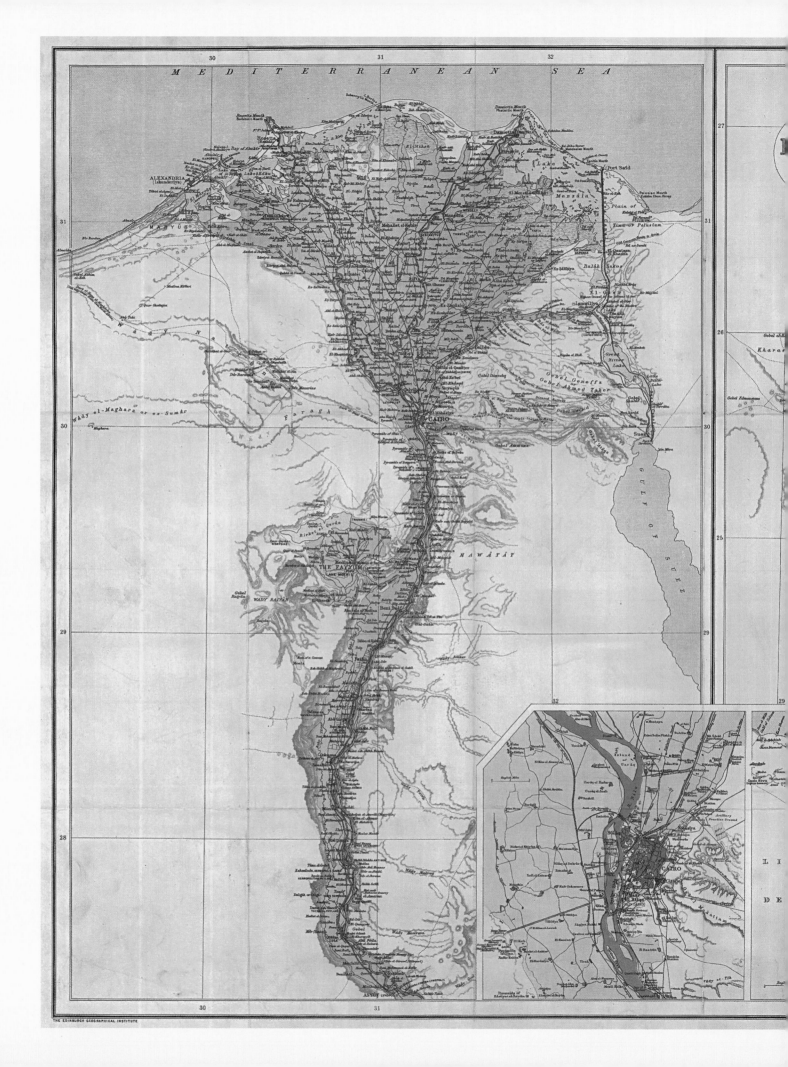

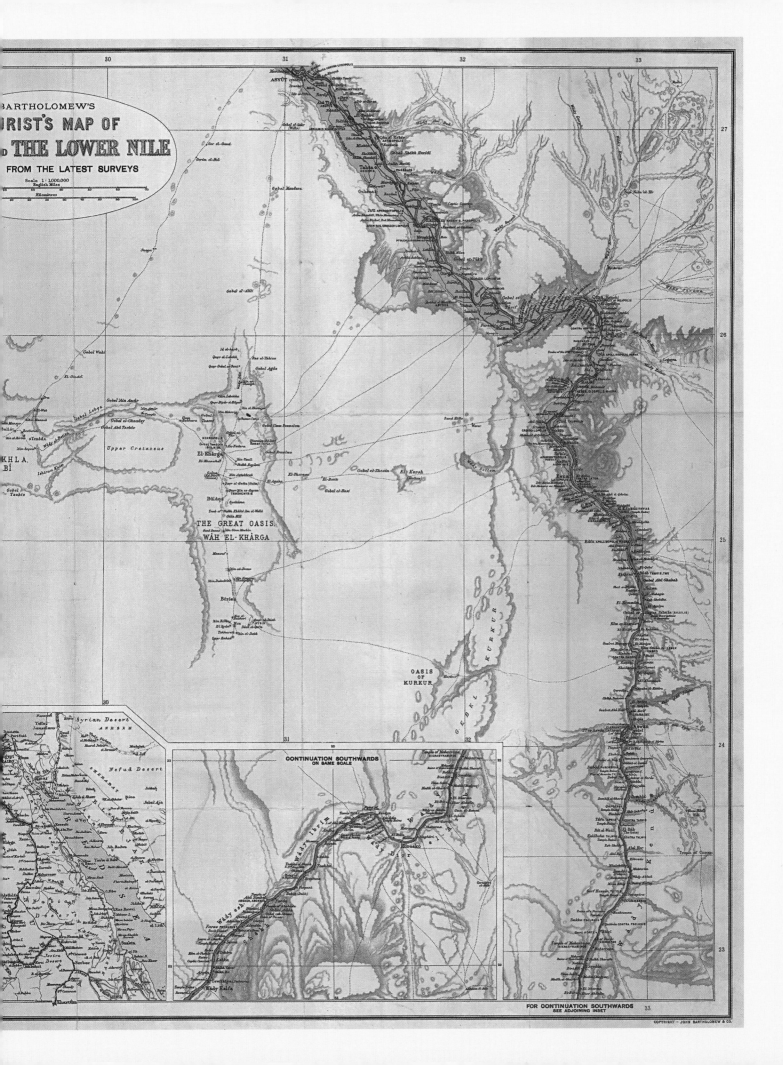

BARTHOLOMEW'S

TOURIST'S MAP OF

THE LOWER NILE

FROM THE LATEST SURVEYS

Scale 1:1,000,000
English Miles

Kilometres

THE GREAT OASIS,
WÂH EL-KHÁRGA

OASIS
OF
KURKUR

OASIS OF KURKUR

CONTINUATION SOUTHWARDS
ON SAME SCALE

FOR CONTINUATION SOUTHWARDS
SEE ADJOINING INSET

The Sphynx is grand in its loneliness; it is imposing in its magnitude; it is impressive in the mystery that hangs over its story. And there is that in the overshadowing majesty of this eternal figure of stone, with its accusing memory of the deeds of all ages, which reveals to one something of what he shall feel when he shall stand at last in the awful presence of God.

A few years before, a very different writer had visited Egypt. The young Gustave Flaubert – he was only 28 – had come in 1850 to gather inspiration from the Orient. His tone was more sardonic and at times salacious than Mark Twain's and he affected a worldly air, but elements of Egypt could still leave him open mouthed:

An astounding hubbub of colour, and your poor old imagination, as if it were at a firework display, is perpetually dazzled. As you go walking along with your mouth open gazing at the minarets covered in white storks, the terraces of the houses where weary slaves are stretching out in the sun, the sections of wall that have sycamores growing through them, the little bells on the dromedaries are tinkling in your ears, and great flocks of black goats are making their way along the street, bleating at the horses, the donkeys, and the merchants.

Flaubert was deeply impressed by the camels which he described as "lurching like turkeys and swaying their necks like swans". But he found the cacophony of noise and colour almost overwhelming:

The detail gets hold of you, grips you tight, squeezes you, and the more engrossing it is the less are you able to take in the ensemble. Then, little by little, it begins to harmonize and fall into place according to the laws of perspective. But for the first few days, may the devil take me, it's an astounding hubbub of colour, and your poor old imagination, as if it were at a firework display, is perpetually dazzled.

At the same time as Flaubert arrived in Egypt, a young Englishwoman was also travelling up the Nile. She was yet to

Left: "Egyptian guides with European tourists". Photographer unknown, 1867. Mark Twain was horrified to see a fellow tourist clambering up the Sphinx with a hammer to knock off a chunk as a souvenir.

Above: "Bartholomew's Tourist's Map of Egypt and the Lower Nile, prepared from the latest surveys", 1897. Detail showing area surrounding Cairo.

Opposite: "Bartholomew's Tourist's Map of Egypt and the Lower Nile, prepared from the latest surveys", 1897, detail.

84

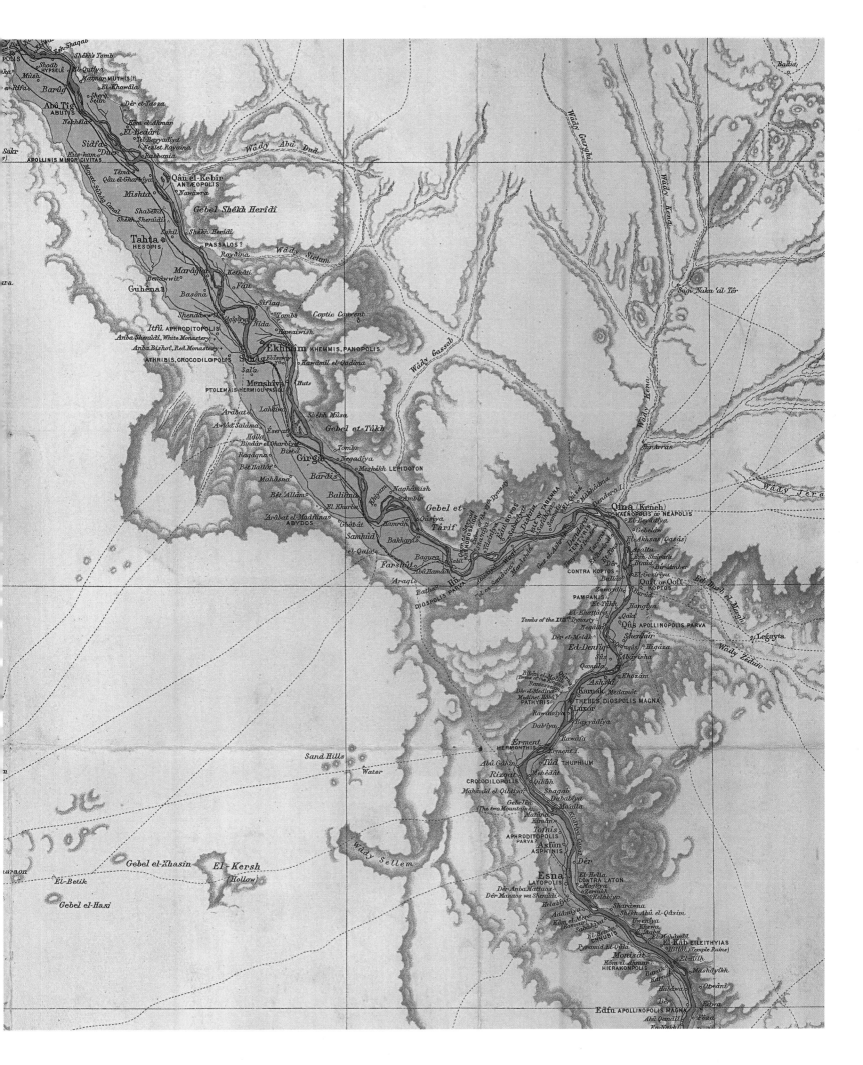

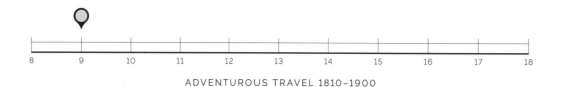
become famous, but for the young Florence Nightingale, Egypt was her first adventure, and her journey there a way of beginning to assert her independence.

"No one ever talks about the beauty of Cairo," she wrote to her family, "or ever gives you the least idea of this surpassing city. I thought it was a place to buy stores at and pass through on one's way to India, instead of its being the rose of cities, the garden of the desert, a pearl of Moorish architecture, the fairest, really the fairest, place of birth below."

She too, like Mark Twain, enjoyed riding the donkeys: "You address your ass in the tenderest terms and in the purist Arabic; you adjure him by all the names of friendship to stop, but he understands no Arabic except the driver's and on he goes full trot while you are making hairbreadth escapes at every corner."

When they rode out through the gates of the city, she had an epiphanic moment surveying the view from the terraced mosque overlooking the Pyramids. She thought of all the biblical figures like Moses and Mary who might have beheld the same view and reflected that while they were dead, "the Nile still flows and the Pyramids stand there still". It was a sentiment that drew many a Victorian traveller to Egypt, often with this Bartholomew's Tourist's Map in their hands.

Below: "La route conduisant aux Pyramides No.4". Photograph by Abdullah Freres, *c.*1870–1900

Opposite: "Mosque el Mooristan". Plate from *Egypt and Nubia from drawings made on the spot* by David Roberts, RA, 1846–49

Following pages: "Cairo, looking west". Plate from *Egypt and Nubia from drawings made on the spot*. "No one ever talks about the beauty of Cairo," Florence Nightingale wrote to her family, "or ever gives you the least idea of this surpassing city."

La Route conduisant aux Pyramides N°4   Abdullah Freres

El Mooristan.
Cairo.

David Roberts R.A.

Cairo looking West

A Sense of Space and Distance

The Geography of the Holy Land

There are many ways of writing a geography of Palestine, and of illustrating the History by the Land, but some are wearisome and some vain. They do not give a vision of the land as a whole, nor help you to hear through it the sound of running history.

(Opening lines to the Preface to George Adam Smith,
The Historical Geography of the Holy Land, 1894)

During the nineteenth century, the Holy Land (or Palestine as it was loosely known) became a place of increasing fascination for Victorian travellers who wanted to trace biblical history, at a time when the evangelical revival encouraged Bible-preaching and Bible-reading.

Between 1869 and 1882, 5,000 tourists did "The Eastern Tour" promoted by Thomas Cook, who was himself an active Baptist. Those who stayed at home could still read about Jerusalem and the geography of Palestine in the many books that fed this appetite. Anthony Trollope commented that there were so many guides to the Holy Land that it had become as accessible and well known to the British reading public as France: "Jerusalem and the Jordan are as common to us as were Paris and the Seine to our grandfathers." (*Travelling Sketches*, 1866)

Previously only enterprising adventurers like the pioneering Lady Hester Stanhope (1776–1839) had gained access to the Holy Land. But now it became possible for many more because, according to historian Maggy Hary:

The Egyptian ruler Muhammad Ali allowed Europeans to expand their religious missionary activity in Palestine and open consulates, which Britain did in 1839. He also introduced tough

policing measures which made the journey through the Holy Land safer for European travellers. When Ottoman rule was re-established in 1840, this policy was continued... Without consuls in Palestine, explorers of the Holy Land would have lacked a protection that was crucial for their inquiry.

(Maggy Hary, "The Holy Land in British Eyes")

The "improving" biblical map illustrated opposite was published in 1841 by Richard Palmer. It was designed to show the journeys of the Israelites both to Egypt and to Mount Sinai. The thin red line shows their wanderings during the years of exile, while the small blue squares reference the biblical narrative, which is listed in the accompanying rubric.

It is typical of a growing tide of such maps, although this example is a particularly fine and detailed one. In 1865, a society was even set up in London with the title of the Palestine Exploration Fund, established expressly "for the accurate and

Opposite: "A map of Arabia Petrea, the Holy Land, and Part of Egypt …" by Richard Palmer, 1841.

Following pages: "General view of Nazareth". Plate from *The Holy Land, Syria, Idumea, Arabia, Egypt and Nubia, from drawings made on the spot* by David Roberts, RA, 1842–43.

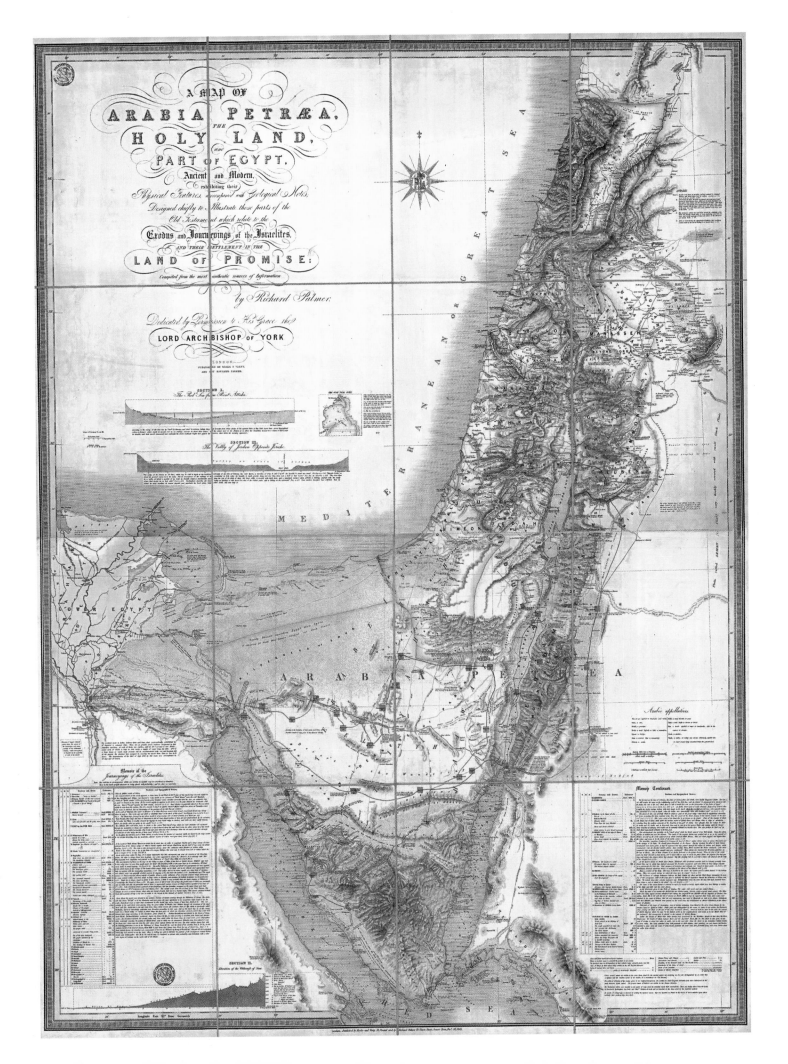

Nazareth April 18th 1859

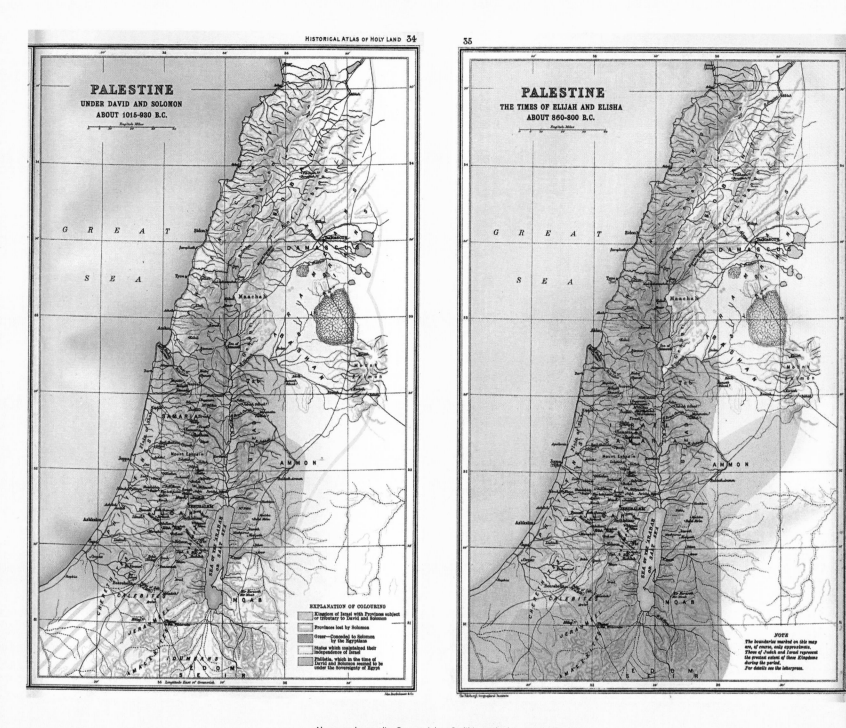

35

PALESTINE

UNDER DAVID AND SOLOMON
ABOUT 1015-930 B.C.

PALESTINE

THE TIMES OF ELIJAH AND ELISHA
ABOUT 860-800 B.C.

Above and opposite: George Adam Smith's meticulous maps of
biblical scholarship were later used to draw up the boundaries for
the new state of Israel. From *Atlas of the Historical Geography of the
Holy Land*, designed and edited by George Adam Smith, 1915.

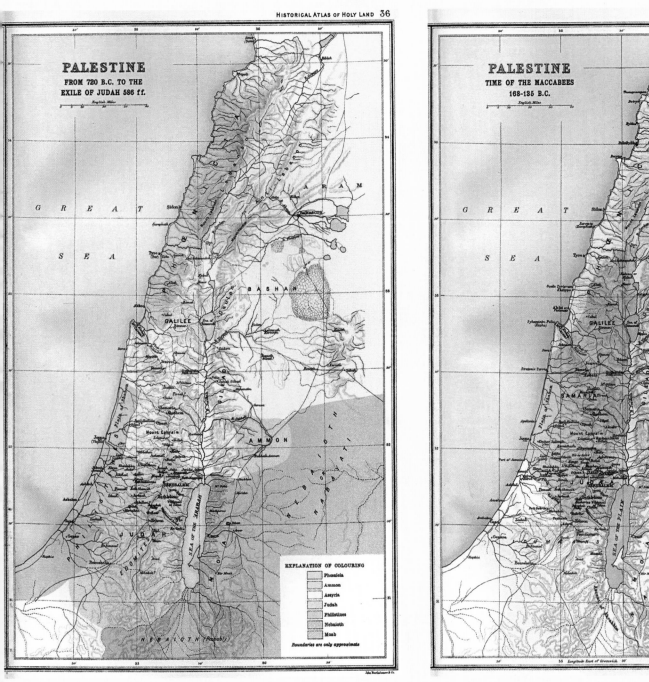

PALESTINE

FROM 720 B.C. TO THE
EXILE OF JUDAH 586 ff.

English Miles

G R E A T

S E A

BASHAN

GALILEE

AMMON

N E B A I O T H   O R   N A B A Y A T I

Mount Ephraim

JERUSALEM

EDOMITES

SEA OF THE ARABAH

N E B A I O T H (Probably)

EXPLANATION OF COLOURING

	Phœnicia
	Ammon
	Assyria
	Judah
	Philistines
	Nebaioth
	Moab

Boundaries are only approximate

John Bartholomew & Co.

PALESTINE

TIME OF THE MACCABEES
168-135 B.C.

English Miles

G R E A T

S E A

GALILEE

BATANÆA

SAMARIA

Mount Ephraim

SEA OF THE PLAIN

EXPLANATION OF COLOURING

	Judæa
	Samaria
	Galilee

Longitude East of Greenwich

John Bartholomew & Co.

systematic investigation of the archaeology, topography, geology and physical geography, and manners and customs of the Holy Land for Biblical Illustration".

However, writing these guidebooks was not always as easy as it sounded. Many of the biblical place names had changed or been lost. For those travellers with a religious interest, it could be very difficult to identify the sites in the countryside outside of the major towns.

Maps like this one helped such adventurous travellers; while the guidebook that towards the end of the nineteenth century became a runaway success was written by a young Scottish minister called George Adam Smith. Despite its dry title, *The*

Historical Geography of the Holy Land was a bestseller and went through no less than 25 editions by 1931.

Adam Smith wrote it as a young man in 1894 and during his long life (1856–1942) continually updated successive versions. Remarkably, it has remained in print ever since, a record few Victorian travel books have achieved.

The Historical Geography of the Holy Land was successful because Adam Smith spent so much time as a young man tramping across modern Israel, Palestine, Jordan and Syria. He also brought formidable levels of biblical scholarship to the task. But above all he had the unusual gift of being able to talk about landscape in a way which made it exciting: a gift

few writers, let alone geography teachers, have been able to master. Despite the author's concerns in the opening line of the Preface, no one could ever say of his book that it was either "wearisome or vain".

He talks, for instance, of the influence of the desert on the Jewish imagination; how the proximity of the desert "gave the ancient natives of Judaea, as it gives the mere visitor to-day,

Opposite: "Palestine under Herod's will and in the time of Christ, 4 BC–37 AD". From *Atlas of the Historical Geography of the Holy Land*, designed and edited by George Adam Smith, 1915.

Above: "Damascas Gate". Plate from *The Holy Land, Syria, Idumea, Arabia, Egypt and Nubia, from drawings made on the spot* by David Roberts, RA, 1842–43.

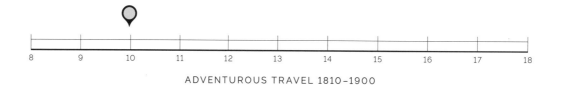
the sense of living next door to doom; the sense of how narrow is the border between life and death." And that how only by travelling right across the Holy Land could you experience "that sense of space and distance, the stupendous contrasts of desert and fertility as you travelled inland from the hard, straight coast with the sea breaking into foam."

But he also has a tremendous ability to conjure up the very ancient history of the land and make it come alive. This tremendous passage has a wonderful verve to it:

One afternoon in 1891, while we were resting in the dale at the foot of Mount Tabor, there passed three great droves of unladen camels. We asked the drivers, "Where are you from?" "Damascus." "And where are you going?" "Jaffa and Gaza; but, if we do not get the camels sold there, we shall drive them down to Egypt."

How ancient a succession these men were following! From Abraham's time, every year that war was not afoot, camels have passed by this road to Egypt …

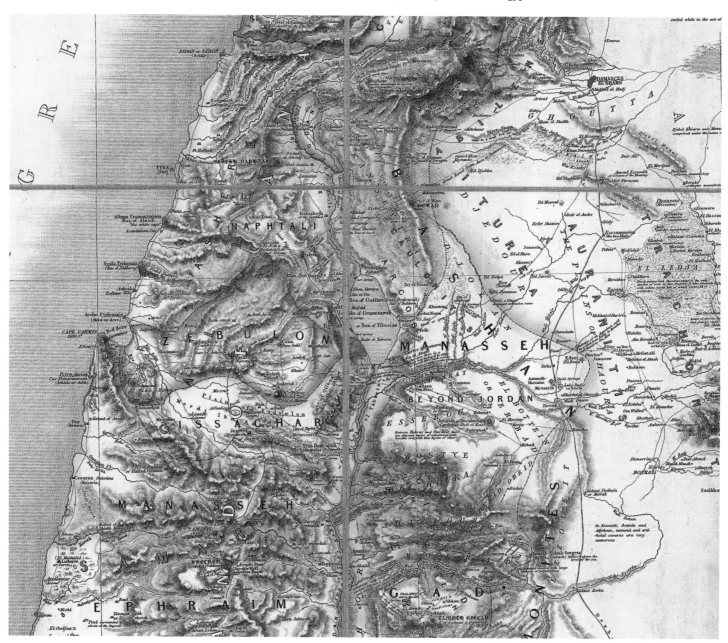

Some years after *The Historical Geography of the Holy Land*, which is a guidebook with a few illustrative maps, Adam Smith decided to do a companion volume, *Atlas of the Historical Geography of the Holy Land* of 1914, comprised solely of historical maps showing how the division of Israel had changed during biblical times.

The book had unintended consequences. When the British under David Lloyd George came to draw up the borders for a new "Jewish Palestine" after the Balfour Declaration, which they did at the San Remo Conference of 1920, they turned to these maps as the only authoritative source for what those historical borders should be. Lloyd George cited Adam Smith as the principal authority on the ancient Holy Land. So the borders of Israel, which at times have been so contentious, were determined by a Scottish biblical scholar – a story which today has become almost forgotten.

Opposite: "A map of Arabia Petrea, the Holy Land, and Part of Egypt … " by Richard Palmer, 1841, detail.

Below: "A map of Arabia Petrea, the Holy Land, and Part of Egypt … " by Richard Palmer, 1841, detail showing area around Sinai.

Following pages: "Descent to the Valley of the Jordan". Plate from *The Holy Land, Syria, Idumea, Arabia, Egypt and Nubia, from drawings made on the spot* by David Roberts, RA, 1842–43.

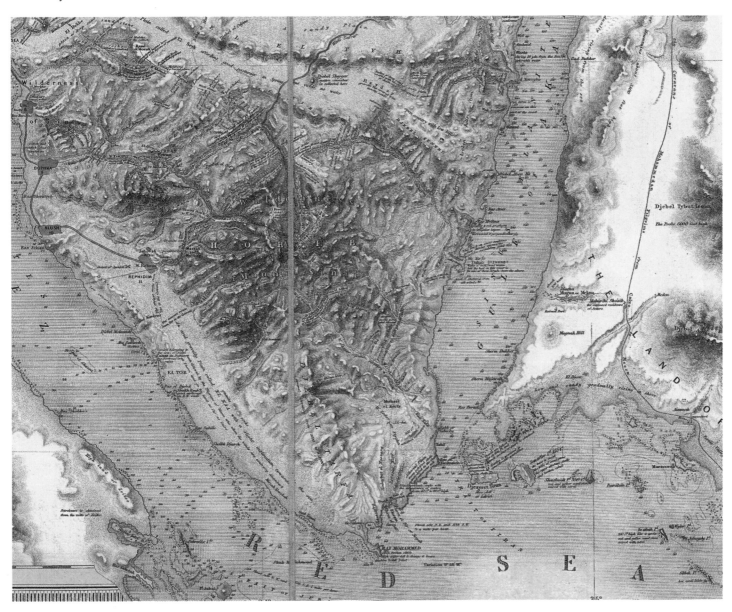

La Serenissima

Venice

*Toward evening, as we sat silent and hardly conscious of where we
were – subdued into that meditative calm that comes so surely after
a conversational storm – someone shouted "VENICE!"*

*And sure enough, afloat on the placid sea a league away, lay a great city, with
its towers and domes and steeples drowsing in a golden mist of sunset.*

(Mark Twain, *The Innocents Abroad*, 1869)

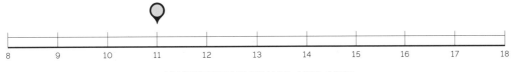

Like many commentators of the nineteenth century, Mark Twain enjoyed the melancholy of what was seen as a decayed empire: "a haughty, invincible, magnificent Republic for nearly fourteen hundred years" reduced now to "a crumbling grandeur of wharves and palaces about her [as] she sits among her stagnant lagoons, forlorn and beggared, forgotten of the world."

"Forgotten of the world" might be putting it strongly, given the amount of tourists, like Mark Twain himself, beating a path to its door. And Twain cast his customarily amused eye across its peculiarities. He describes the gondola that first meets them on their night-time arrival as looking more like a hearse and the gondolier himself as a caterwauling guttersnipe. But just when he feels that the Venice of old must have disappeared, he is swept into the Grand Canal:

Under the mellow moonlight, the Venice of poetry and romance stood revealed. Right from the water's edge rose long lines of stately palaces of marble; gondolas were gliding swiftly hither and thither and disappearing suddenly through unsuspected gates and alleys; ponderous stone bridges threw their shadows athwart the glittering waves.

There was life and motion everywhere, and yet everywhere there was a hush, a stealthy sort of stillness, that was suggestive of secret enterprises of bravoes and of lovers; and clad half

Opposite: "Venezia – Palazzo Ducale Veduta Generale". Photographer unknown, *c.*1880.

Above: "Grand Canal, Venice". Photographer unknown, *c.*1870–73. Mark Twain described the gondola that first met them on their night-time arrival as looking more like a hearse and the gondolier himself as a caterwauling guttersnipe.

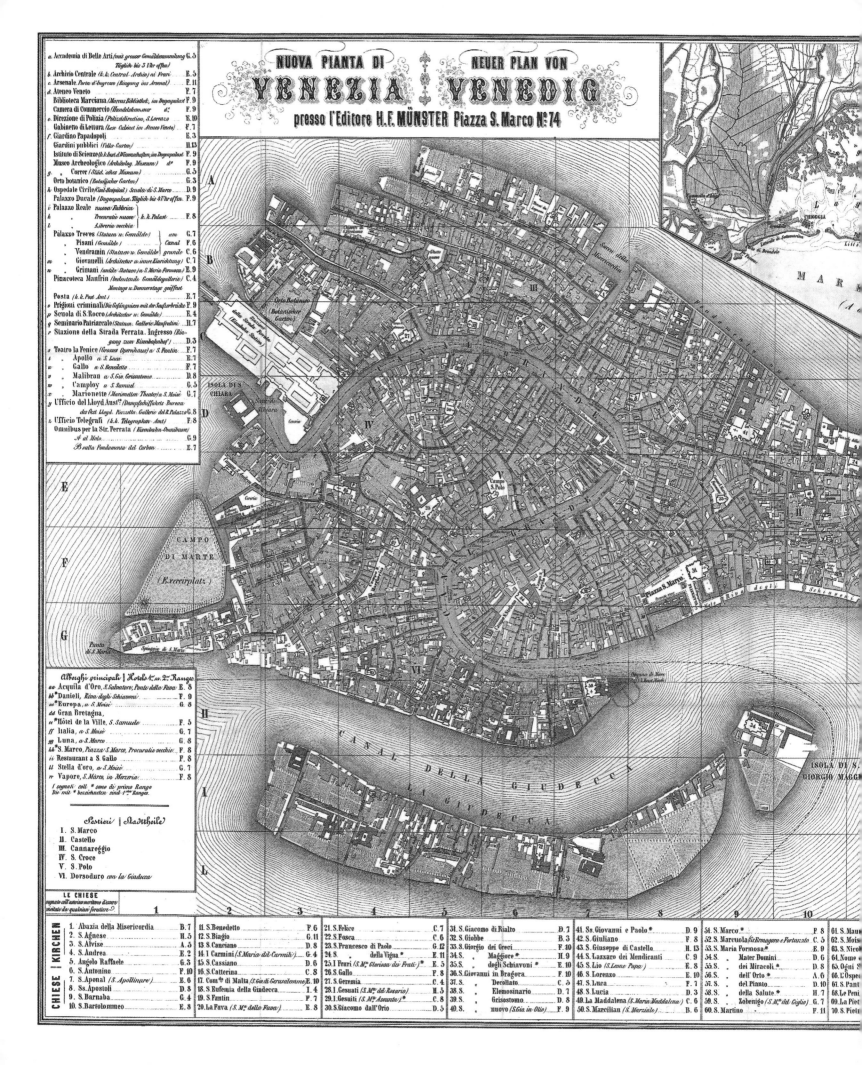

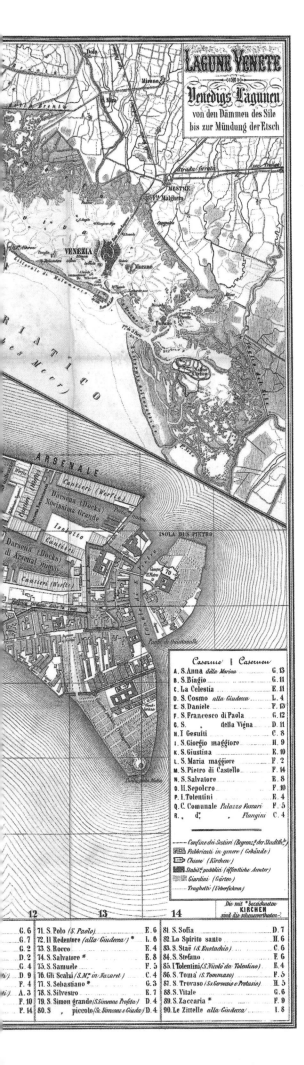

*in moonbeams and half in mysterious shadows, the grim old
mansions of the Republic seemed to have an expression about
them of having an eye out for just such enterprises as these at
that same moment. Music came floating over the waters –
Venice was complete.*

Twain preferred Venice by night. During the day he, like
so many other visitors, found the city could be hard work.
For a start, he complained, "there were no sidewalks worth
mentioning".

Many of his fellow nineteenth-century tourists had been
inspired to come by Turner's famous pictures of the city. The
artist only spent about four weeks in Venice overall, but devoted
most of his final years to turning the results of those visits into
some of his finest paintings. His series of views of the Lagoon
turn the city into an almost abstract meditation on light, colour
and the reflective surfaces of water and stone.

It is therefore not surprising that John Ruskin, Turner's great
promoter, should also have had such a lifelong engagement with
Venice. He first visited the city with his parents when he was only
16 and henceforth declared himself – perhaps tactlessly – to be
"a foster child of Venice". He certainly wrote over half a million
words about the place. His *The Stones of Venice*, published in three
volumes between 1851 and 1853, weighs as heavily as it sounds,
but contains some of his finest writing.

Ruskin was fascinated by the interplay between Byzantine,
Gothic and Renaissance architecture in the city. He also
celebrated imperfection – a radical idea for the Victorians – going
so far as to declare that the imperfections in Venetian architecture
were "in some sort essential to all that we know in life."

He recorded the city in minute detail, not just with his
writing, but also with sketches and even photography (by 1849
he had managed to get hold of an early camera so that he could
take daguerrotypes). The book was so influential that by the end
of the century, Marcel Proust's narrator in *À la Recherche du Temps
Perdu* feels he has to visit Venice because he has been inspired by
Ruskin.

This map (left) published by H. F. Munster in 1854 and almost
contemporary with Ruskin's *The Stones of Venice* was clearly
designed for the tourist of that day who wished to visit the many

Left: "Nuova Pianta della R. Citta di Venezia".
Published: Venice: H. F. Munster, 1854.

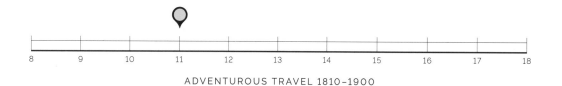

churches. It is of course remarkable how little has changed since that time; a modern visitor could use it equally well.

Mark Twain, however, remained more resistant to the charms of Venetian architecture:

Of course we went to see the venerable relic of the ancient glory of Venice, with its pavements worn and broken by the passing feet of a thousand years of plebeians and patricians – The Cathedral of St. Mark ... I could not go into ecstasies over its coarse mosaics, its unlovely Byzantine architecture, or its five hundred curious interior columns from as many distant quarries.

One suspects this sort of comment would have given Ruskin one of his fits of hysterics (he was once laid prostrate by such a fit at the sight of a particular Tintoretto). But Twain was proud to proclaim that from the moment of arrival, he was more interested in the skill of the gondolier than the palaces they passed. The American describes how the gondolas took him flying down the great canals at such speed that he could glimpse into the front door of the palaces, and would then slow

Above: "Venezia – Molo dal Ponte della Pietá". Photographer unknown, *c.*1880.

Opposite: "Canal, Venice". Photographer unknown, *c.*1870–73.

down to move to "a spirit of grave meditation" through the back canals:

We have been in a half-waking sort of dream all the time. I do not know how else to describe the feeling. A part of our being has remained still in the nineteenth century, while another part of it has seemed in some unaccountable way walking among the phantoms of the tenth.

One could argue that Twain's reaction to Venice was a more common if less elevated one that Ruskin's. Were not many other tourists then and later overwhelmed by the sheer profusion of Venetian paintings and churches? Ruskin writes in some detail

about at least 80 churches. Twain claims, with only a touch of exaggeration, that there are 1,500 works by Tintoretto in Venice – and felt he had seen enough pictures of martyrs and saints "to regenerate the world".

But Venice also captivated him and when he finally left, he paid a fond tribute: "We depart to-morrow, and leave the venerable Queen of the Republics to summon her vanished ships, and marshal her shadowy armies, and know again in dreams the pride of her old renown."

Opposite, above: "St Mark's, Venice". Photographer unknown, *c*.1900. Ruskin's *The Stones of Venice* encouraged travellers from all over Europe to come to the city.

Opposite, below: "Rialto Bridge, Venice". Photographer unknown, *c*.1870–73.

Above: "Venezia – Canal Interno S. Catterina". Photographer unknown, *c*.1880.

The Alhambra

The nineteenth century saw a resurgence of romantic interest in the old Moorish ruins of southern Spain, and particularly in the Alhambra palace of Granada. Writers like Washington Irving extolled the Alhambra's virtues in his romantic history of 1829, *The Conquest of Granada,* and championed its preservation:

> *Such was [the Alhambra's] lavish splendor that even at the present day the stranger, wandering through its silent courts and deserted halls, gazes with astonishment at gilded ceilings and fretted domes, the brilliancy and beauty of which have survived the vicissitudes of war and the silent dilapidation of age.*

A well deserved memorial has been erected to Irving in the grounds of the palace. Before him, both the building and the campaign to regain it had been largely forgotten as a mere "end-note" to a phase of Spanish history.

That said, he also embellished his account with abandon. On the evidence of some red staining of a marble basin, he invented a tale of a terrible massacre that had taken place within the walls. His Victorian readers lapped up such descriptions.

It was remarkable that so much had survived for Irving to see, as the palace's fortunes were mixed after the *Reconquista* of 1492 when the Moors were expelled from Spain. After some initial conservation, there had been long centuries of neglect.

The Catholic monarchs Ferdinand and Isabella preserved it as a symbol of their victory over the Moors – and in the same month that they deposed Boabdil, the last Muslim ruler of Andalucia, they gave an audience at the Alhambra to an adventurous explorer called Christopher Columbus who wanted to sail across the Atlantic. Their successor Charles V built his own palace within the walls.

After that, the Alhambra fell into benign neglect and was variously used as an asylum for debtors and invalid soldiers, a prison for convicts and galley-slaves, a silk factory, a powder magazine, a salt-fish store and a pen for donkeys and sheep. The French ransacked it during the Napoleonic occupation.

Irving celebrated the elegiac nature of the deserted palace. He retold the famous story of how when Boabdil was forced to leave both the Alhambra and Spain by Ferdinand and Isabella, he crossed a pass in the Alpujarras mountains below Granada on the way to the coast, a pass which later became known as "the Moor's last sigh". He is said to have looked back longingly at the

Above: Washington Irving. Illustration from *Astoria, or, Enterprise Beyond the Rocky Mountains* by Washington Irving, 1839.

Opposite, above: "Patio de los Leones". Photograph by Ayola, *c.*1880. Writers like Washington Irving extolled the Alhambra's virtues in his romantic history of 1829, *The Conquest of Granada.*

Opposite, below: "Plan of the Palace of the Alhambra". From *Murray's A Handbook for Travellers in Spain,* 1888.

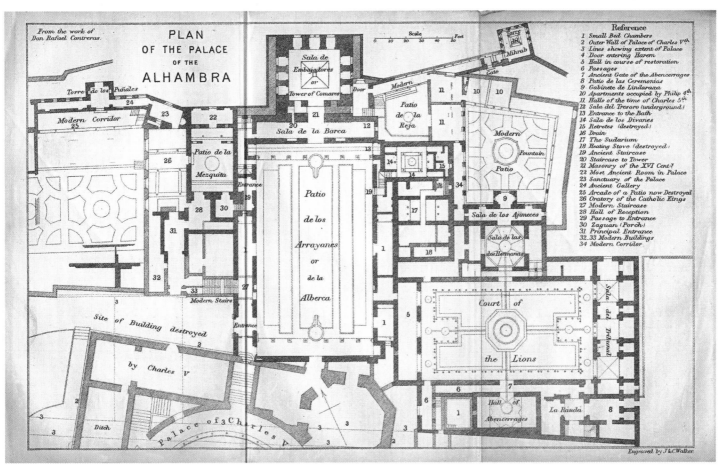

PLAN
OF THE PALACE
OF THE
ALHAMBRA

Scale
0 10 20 30 40 50 Feet

Torre de los
Picos

Mihrab

Gate

Modern

Door

Torre de los Peñales
24
23
22

Modern Corridor
25

Patio
de la
Reja

11

10

10

Patio de la
Mezquita
26

21

20

Sala de la Barca

12

Entrance
29

28   30

31

Modern
Fountain
Patio

Patio
de los
Arrayanes
or
de la
Alberca

14

15

19

18

34

Sala de los Ajimeces

32

33

27

Modern Stairs

Entrance

Sala de las
dos Hermanas

Court   of
the   Lions

Sala
del
Tribunal

Site of Building destroyed

by Charles V

Ditch

Palace of Charles V

5

6   7

6   1

Hall of
Abencerrages

La Rauda

8

Engraved by J.&C.Walker.

Reference

1 Small Bed. Chambers
2 Outer Wall of Palace of Charles V.th
3 Lines shewing extent of Palace
4 Door entering Harem
5 Hall in course of restoration
6 Passages
7 Ancient Gate of the Abencerrages
8 Patio de las Ceremonias
9 Gabinete de Lindaraxa
10 Apartments occupied by Philip 4.th
11 Halls of the time of Charles 5.th
12 Sala del Tresoro (underground)
13 Entrance to the Bath
14 Sala de los Divanes
15 Retretes (destroyed)
16 Drain
17 The Sudarium
18 Heating Stove (destroyed)
19 Ancient Staircase
20 Staircase to Tower
21 Masonry of the XVI Cent.y
22 Most Ancient Room in Palace
23 Sanctuary of the Palace
24 Ancient Gallery
25 Arcade of a Patio now Destroyed
26 Oratory of the Catholic Kings
27 Modern Staircase
28 Hall of Reception
29 Passage to Entrance
30 Zaguan (Porch)
31 Principal Entrance
32.33 Modern Buildings
34 Modern Corridor

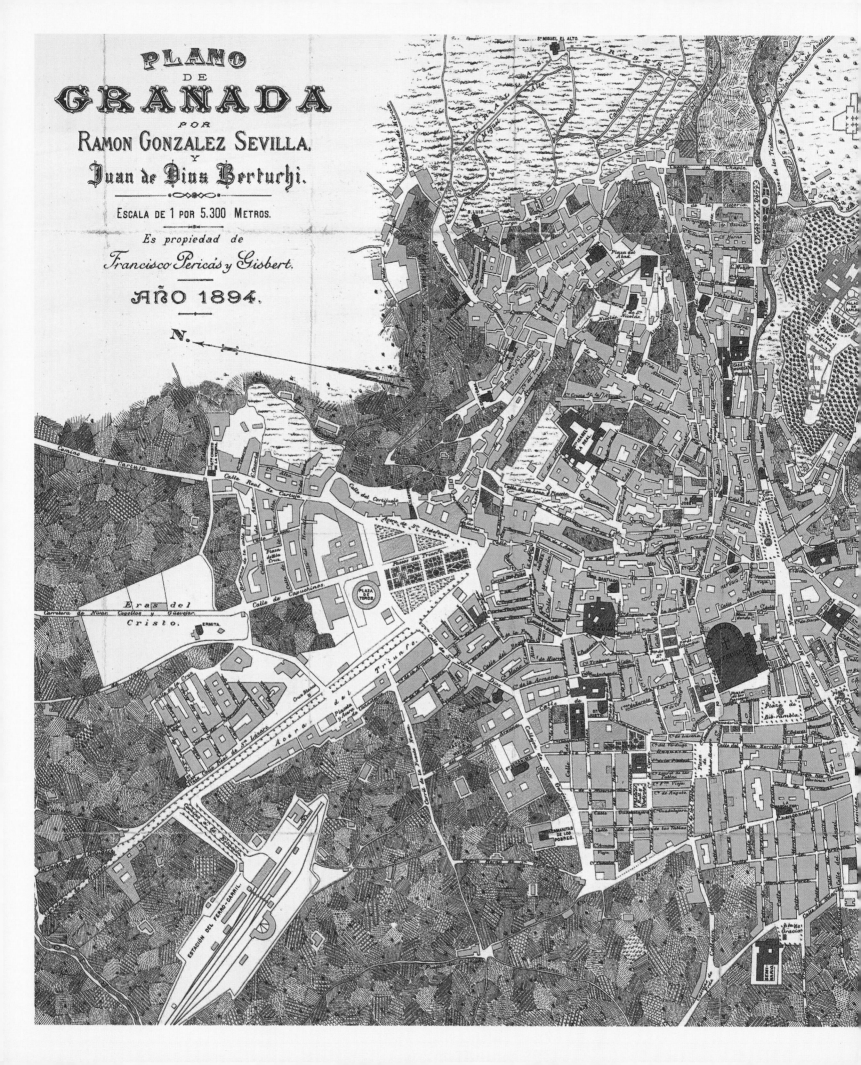

wonderful buildings and been reproved by his mother, who told him: "Now you weep like a woman over what you could not defend as a man."

The Alhambra was a military redoubt when it was built, with the shadow of the Castilian kings to the north falling heavily on the massive walls, which explains their strongly fortified and not particularly attractive nature. But inside, a series of courtyards contrasted the simplicity of Islamic garden design with elaborately executed calligraphy and decorative work of the highest order.

There was much to entrance the other nineteenth-century writers who followed Irving. A long pool ran down the Court of the Myrtles and at the end was a display of the carved Islamic plasterwork known as *sebka*, with its foliage and flowers. They could imagine how the Sultan would have sat in the Hall of the Ambassadors, under a dome inlaid with mother-of-pearl and a night sky showing the seven Islamic heavens.

The view through to the courtyard fountain ringed by the 12 stone lions that give the Patio of the Lions its name was through a forest of pillared friezes so elaborate that Alexander Dumas (1802–70) described it as "a dream turned to stone by a magician's wand". The French novelist also gave the Alhambra a terrific epigram: "I begin to think that there is only one greater pleasure than to see Granada; and that is to see her again."

The Italian author Edmondo de Amicis went even further in *Cuore* (1886), when he described the building's architecture as expressive of "love and voluptuousness: love with its mysteries, caprices, expansions and its bursts of gratitude to God; voluptuousness with its melancholy and silence."

The palace's "rediscovery" in the nineteenth century was driven by the urge towards both romanticism and orientalism, a heady combination; but the site was also carefully documented by nineteenth-century architects and designers like Owen Jones and Jules Goury, as well as the photographer Charles Clifford. Because of its easy accessibility, the Alhambra became a reference point for the many pastiches of Islamic architecture that sprang up as hotels, theatres and cinemas across the Western world, often bearing the Alhambra's name; even though it represented a very particular moment in Islamic architecture – some would say a decadent last flowering.

Left: "Plano de Granada" by Ramon Gonzalez Sevilla, 1894.

THE MINERVA LIBRARY OF FAMOUS BOOKS.
Edited by G. T. BETTANY, *M.A., B.Sc.*

THE BIBLE IN SPAIN

OR, THE

JOURNEYS, ADVENTURES, AND IMPRISONMENTS
OF AN ENGLISHMAN,

IN

AN ATTEMPT TO CIRCULATE THE SCRIPTURES
IN THE PENINSULA.

BY

GEORGE BORROW,

AUTHOR OF
"THE GIPSIES OF SPAIN."

WITH A BIOGRAPHICAL INTRODUCTION.

SECOND EDITION.

WARD, LOCK, AND CO.,
LONDON, NEW YORK, AND MELBOURNE.
1889.

Mark Twain decided not to visit the Alhambra, pleading that the 16-hour coach ride to Granada was too much, and instead proclaimed the attractions of the Moorish palace of the Alcázar in Seville in similar terms: "I cannot describe it. In my memory, its courts and gardens will always be a hasheesh delusion, its Hall of Ambassadors a marvellous dream."

Andalucia may have attracted most attention, but George Borrow's book of 1843, *The Bible in Spain*, ostensibly a story of how he had tried to sell Bibles right across it, brought the whole country into focus; moreover it was "a song of wild Spain" which celebrated the gypsies, muleteers and oriental influences. The book was so popular that it sold 10,000 copies within four months, and went into many editions throughout the nineteenth century, both in Britain and in the United States.

The seeds of Spain's huge success as a tourist destination today were sown a century ago by those Victorian writers who eulogized the romance of forgotten monuments such as the Alhambra and the Moorish traditions it enshrined. This map (pp.112–13) bears testimony to their exploration both of a country and of what was to them a lost and exotic past.

Opposite: "Alhambra, Granada. Sala del Reposos del Bano". Photograph by Garzón, *c.*1880. The palace's "rediscovery" in the nineteenth century was driven by the urge towards both romanticism and orientalism, a heady combination.

Above: Frontispiece illustration and title page of *The Bible in Spain, or, the Journeys, Adventures, and Imprisonments of an Englishman in an Attempt to Circulate the Scriptures in the Peninsula* by George Borrow, 1889, 2nd edition. George Borrow's book, ostensibly a story of how he had tried to sell Bibles there, brought the whole country into focus.

Scrambles Amongst the Alps

The opening up of the Alps for regular tourists in the nineteenth century meant a wave of travellers could experience the mountains in a way that previously only explorers had been able. Given that William Wordsworth and the other romantic poets had generated a huge appetite for the appreciation of such wild landscape, the Victorians seized on the opportunity with gusto.

Thomas Cook's first tour to the Alps in 1863 enabled a pioneering group of 60 British tourists to journey up the Rhône Valley south-east from Lake Geneva towards the Mont Blanc massif. It was so successful that many subsequent trips ensued. By the 1880s, Switzerland was receiving a million foreign travellers a year.

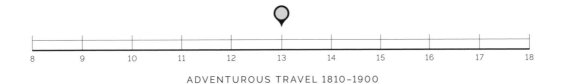

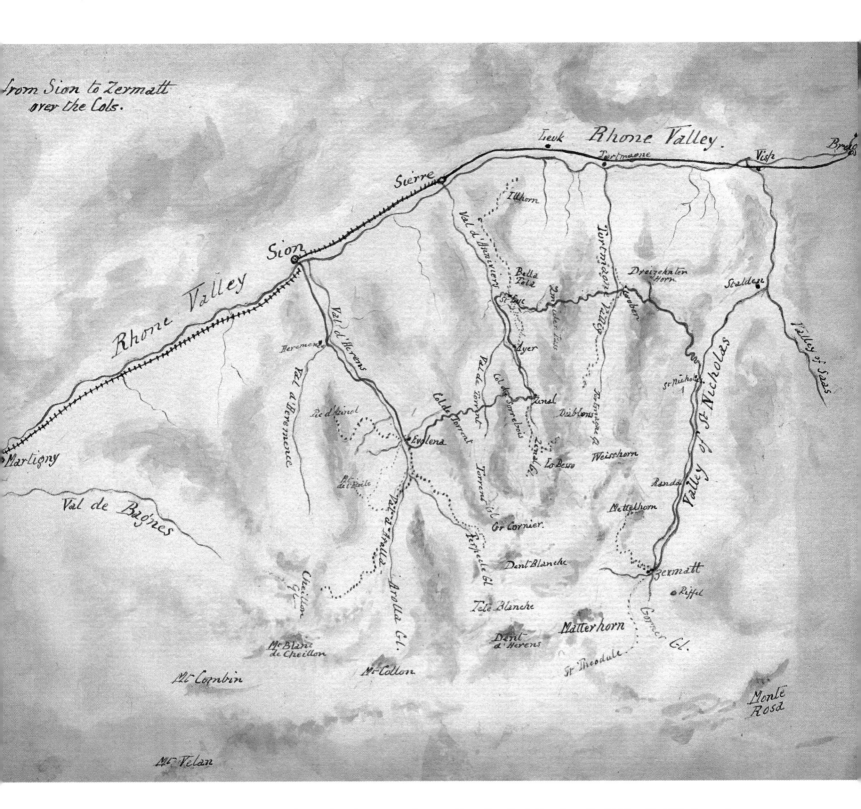

From Sion to Zermatt over the Cols.

Rhone Valley.

Leuk

Tortmagne

Visp

Brato

Sierre

Illhorn

Val d'Anniviers

Bella Tola

Turtmann Valley

Dreizehnten Horn

Staldeu

Sion

Rhone Valley

Martigny

Val de Bagnes

Heremens

Val d'Herens

Val d'Herenence

Pic d'Arrel

Pt de l'Etoile

Pic d'Arrel

Evolena

Col de Torrent

Col de Torrent

Col de Sorrebois

Zinal

Diablons

St Luc

Ayer

Val de Tourtz

Zmutter Thal

Zinaler

Lo Besso

Weisshorn

St Nicholas

Randa

Mettelhorn

Valley of St Nicholas

Valley of Saas

Cheillon Gl.

Arolla Gl.

Torrend Gl.

Gr Cornier.

Rothecke Gl.

Dent Blanche

Tete Blanche

Dent d'Herens

Matterhorn

St Theodule

Gorner Gl.

Zermatt

Riffel

Mt Blanc de Cheillon

Mt Collon

Mt Combin

Monte Rosa

Mt Velan

Opposite: Late nineteenth-century climbers in the Alps. Photographer unknown, c.1880–1900. By the end of the century tourists were coming to the Alps in droves.

Above: "From Sion to Zermatt over the Cols". From *The Middle Passage from Sion to Zermatt, August 1863, II*, a manuscript diary by Jane Freshfield, 1863.

Cook's first customers reached Geneva by train, but afterwards had to travel on by either carriage or mule – although this soon changed as better roads and more railways helped ease access. By 1891, one could even travel by train all the way to the remote village of Zermatt, nestled under the Matterhorn; and then, seven years later, take a pioneering rack-and-pinion railway, the Gornergrat, up a steep gradient to a glacier and stay in the imposing Riffelalp hotel at over 7,000 ft.

The traveller today to these high alpine villages is often surprised by the large Victorian and Edwardian hotels built for this English market, not just in Zermatt – where one might expect it – but on high remote areas of the Val d'Anniviers, like the Hotel Weisshorn which still sits on a prominent hilltop some 2,000 feet above the small village of St Luc.

This striking and large hotel was completed in 1891, with four floors, a veranda on stilts – typical for such hotels so that the view could be admired – a formal dining area and a smoking room. The transportation of all the materials had to be provided by mules, while the piano was carried up on the back of six men.

Opposite: Late nineteenth-century climber in the Alps. Photographer unknown, c.1880–1900. A Victorian lady promenading on the ice.

Above: "The Matterhorn – from St Luc–Val d'Anniviers". Pencil sketch from *The Middle Passage from Sion to Zermatt, August 1863. II*, a manuscript diary by Jane Freshfield, 1863.

Left: Jane Freshfield (1814–1901). She travelled out to the Alps on a regular basis during the 1860s, producing both maps and sketches.

The map shown on p.117 was drawn by Jane Freshfield (1814–1901), who travelled out with her husband and son to the Alps on a regular basis during the 1860s. It is of the area just south of the upper Rhône Valley and shows some of the main trekking routes in the area, none of which involved any great mountaineering skill.

The red line shows a route travelling up the Val d'Hérens from the railway station at Sion and then crossing the pass from Evolène to Zinal, which, like Zermatt, had then become one of the principal destinations for British travellers, although now it is less visited.

The route her family took is similar to the "Walkers' Haute Route" that still leads across the high mountain passes between Chamonix and Zermatt. Just as today, it continued for the Freshfields from Zinal across the pass about St Luc that was soon to have the Hotel Weisshorn, and came to Gruben in the small transhumant valley of Turtmanntal, used at that time only for summer pastures.

Jane Freshfield wrote a book, *Alpine Byways*, extolling the pleasures of such Alpine wanderings; a book that set a precedent for other pioneering women travellers, including Janet Adam Smith, literary editor of the *New Statesman*, whose *Mountain Holidays* of 1946 showed how the tradition of literary Alpine wandering in much the same part of the Valais continued right into the twentieth century.

That literary tradition was much enhanced by the quality of some of the early travel and climbing books produced, particularly by Leslie Stephen's *The Playground of Europe* in 1871. Stephen, the father of Virginia Woolf and Vanessa Bell, also went to the small valley of the Turtmanntal, from which he could admire the Weisshorn: "Nowhere have I seen a more delicate combination of mountain massiveness, with soaring and delicately carved pinnacles pushed to the verge of extravagance."

But the book about this area of Switzerland which excited most attention – and some controversy – was Edward Whymper's *Scrambles Amongst the Alps*, also published in 1871, just as tourism was opening up.

This presented nowhere near as romanticized or idealized a picture of the Alps as his contemporaries. On arriving at Zinal, Whymper wanted to find a more direct route to Zermatt across the glaciers that lay between them. To do so, he needed to stay at a mountain hut, which he described in unflattering terms:

… a hovel, growing, as it were, out of the hill-side; roofed with rough slabs of slaty stone; without a door or window; surrounded by quagmires of ordure, and dirt of every description. A foul native invited us to enter. The interior was dark; but, when our eyes became accustomed to the gloom, we saw that our palace was in plan about 15 by 20 feet; on one side it was scarcely five feet high, but on the other was nearly seven. On this side there was a raised platform, about six feet wide, littered with dirty straw and still dirtier sheepskins. This was the bedroom.

(Edward Whymper, *Scrambles Amongst The Alps in the Years 1860–69*)

Above: "Edward Whymper, at the age of 25", from *Scrambles Amongst the Alps* by Edward Whymper, 1936, 6th edition. A complicated, driven man; unlike the often aristocratic members of the Alpine Club, he was a middle-class engraver drawn to the Alps by a compulsion to succeed.

Opposite: Title page from *Scrambles Amongst the Alps in the Years 1860–69* by Edward Whymper, 1871.

SCRAMBLES

AMONGST THE ALPS IN THE

YEARS 1860-69

BY

EDWARD WHYMPER

WITH MAPS AND ILLUSTRATIONS

Toil and pleasure, in their natures opposite, are yet linked together
in a kind of necessary connection.—LIVY.

SECOND EDITION

LONDON

JOHN MURRAY, ALBEMARLE STREET

1871

Edward Whymper was a complicated, driven man. Unlike the often aristocratic members of the Alpine Club, he was a middle-class engraver drawn to the Alps by a compulsion to succeed and to show that while some climbers might be gentlemen amateurs, he was, by comparison, a professional who would stop at nothing to get to a summit.

The summit that commanded all his attention and the main subject of his book was of course the Matterhorn, the most striking, if not the tallest, of the mountains in this part of the Valais.

In 1865, desperate to put a British team together to make the first ascent of the mountain when he realized the Italians were trying to do so from the other side, he enrolled one of the new British travellers as a member of his climbing party. Douglas Hadow was only 19 and this was his first trip to the Alps. While he had done some climbing, he was hopelessly inexperienced for a first ascent of the Matterhorn. Although they successfully summited, Hadow fell as they descended to Zermatt, dragging half the party to their deaths. Whymper and two of the guides survived because a rope linking them with the others broke.

While an age of tourism meant that the Alps had become a more democratic experience, the dangers that they represented had not diminished. Many more British climbers and travellers were to die on the Matterhorn in the years to come, and the cemetery at the English Church in Zermatt is full of their graves.

Opposite: "A cannonade on the Matterhorn (1862)". Illustration from *Scrambles Amongst the Alps* by Edward Whymper, 1871. The book caused a sensation when it was published.

Above: "Hotel du Mont Rose, Zermatt". Illustration from *The Valley of Zermatt and the Matterhorn, a Guide* by Edward Whymper, 1897

Below: "The Riffelalp Hotel". Illustration from *The Valley of Zermatt and the Matterhorn, a Guide* by Edward Whymper, 1897. The traveller today to these high Alpine villages is often surprised by the large Victorian and Edwardian hotels built for the English market.

Following pages: "The Matterhorn from near the summit of the Theodule Pass". Illustration from *Scrambles Amongst the Alps* by Edward Whymper, 1871. The summit that commanded all his attention and the main subject of his book was the Matterhorn, the most striking, if not the tallest, of the mountains in this part of the Valais.

The Teardrop Island

The teardrop island of Ceylon – now Sri Lanka – has long exercised a fascination for travellers. Marco Polo came here, as did the great Arab explorer, Ibn Battuta.

At the very centre of Ceylon, in the middle of the mountains, lay the remote town of Kandy. When this map was published, the jungle was so close to the town that at night leopards would sometimes stroll down the streets at night, drinking at the pools and eating the dogs.

The old kingdom of Kandy still had a mystique about it: Sri Lanka's Shangri-La. For years it had held out against the Portuguese (1505-1658) and the Dutch (1638-1803), only to fall at last to the British, in 1815. The size of Cornwall, it sat at the heart of the island, and the secret of its independence

Above: "Drying tea leaves, Ceylon". Early lantern slide, photographer unknown, c.1880–1900.

Opposite: "Map of the Island of Ceylon", by A. M. Ferguson, 1875.

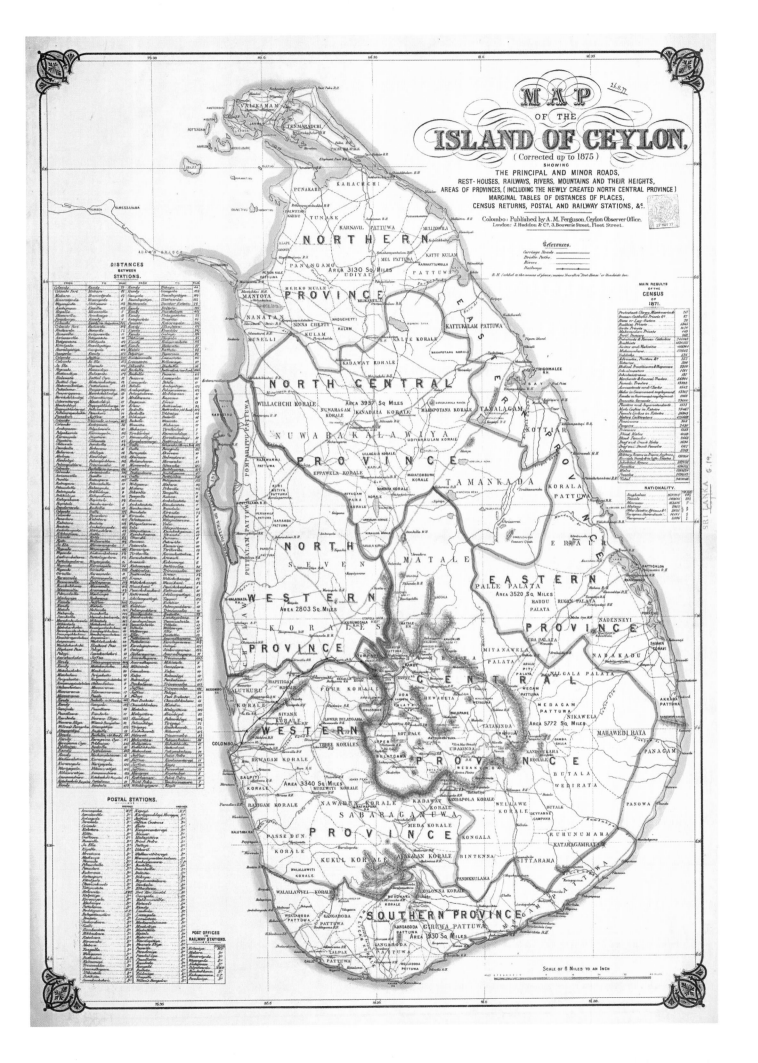

MAP OF THE ISLAND OF CEYLON,

(Corrected up to 1875)

SHOWING

THE PRINCIPAL AND MINOR ROADS,
REST-HOUSES, RAILWAYS, RIVERS, MOUNTAINS AND THEIR HEIGHTS,
AREAS OF PROVINCES, (INCLUDING THE NEWLY CREATED NORTH CENTRAL PROVINCE)
MARGINAL TABLES OF DISTANCES OF PLACES,
CENSUS RETURNS, POSTAL AND RAILWAY STATIONS, &c.

Colombo: Published by A. M. Ferguson, Ceylon Observer Office.
London: J. Haddon & Cº, 3, Bouverie Street, Fleet Street.

References.

Carriage Roads
Bridle Paths
Rivers
Railways

R.H. (added to the names of places) means Travellers' Rest-House' or Roadside Inn.

SCALE OF 8 MILES TO AN INCH

DISTANCES BETWEEN STATIONS.

MAIN RESULTS OF THE CENSUS OF 1871.

NATIONALITY.

POSTAL STATIONS.

POST OFFICES in RAILWAY STATIONS.

was simple: gradient. The mountains around it made for a magnificent natural fortress, rising to 7,000 feet and spouting the wildest of rivers.

The kingdom was Buddhist and one of its most prized relics was the tooth of the Buddha, displayed in the lakeside town of Kandy at the Temple of the Tooth.

Not long after this map (see p.127) was published, the German writer Hermann Hesse arrived in Sri Lanka. It was 1911, and Hesse, aged 34, was just at the beginning of his own long journey to the East which would result in his classic and influential account of Buddhist thought, *Siddharta*.

Already fascinated by Buddhism, he travelled to Kandy in the centre of the mountainous interior. A priest led him into one of the inner sanctums where, as his eyes grew accustomed to the dark, he was able to make out the enormous reclining figure of a huge Buddha filling the cave. In his notebook he commented that he had the overwhelming impression that "should the Buddha rise, the entire mountain would collapse down upon us."

When he wandered along the lake, he was struck by the image of a blind old man who stepped off the ferry and was led to the temple; an image he may have returned to in *Siddharta* when one of the most famous passages relates to the time the main character, Siddharta, spends with an old ferryman. From him, he learns to "listen to the river" and to be content.

Hesse always believed that you needed fully to experience worldly pleasures before you could appreciate the austerity of any spiritual retreat. His heroes Narziss and Goldmund wrestle with this contradiction, as does the hero himself in *Siddharta*.

His time in Sri Lanka exemplified this seeming contradiction: finding it difficult to assimilate the East, he partook of a great deal of wine and opium in Kandy and was in the middle of a delirium of dysentery and decadence when he set off to cleanse his thoughts and climb a mountain.

He chose to summit nearby Pidurutalagala, and see "deep blue and immense, the entire high mountain system of Ceylon piled up in mighty walls, and in its midst the beautiful, ancient, and holy pyramid of Adam's Peak" (*Aus Indien*, 1913).

It was one of his last days in the subcontinent before he

Right: "Giant Banyan trees in Ceylon". Photograph by B. F. K. Rives, 1880–90.

Next spread: "A ruined Buddhist temple carved from rock at Anuradhapura, Ceylon". Photograph by Skeen & Co., 1880–90. Hesse was determined to view the landscape of the East without sentimental mysticism or what we would now call "orientalism".

returned to Europe and he wanted "to bid India a proper and dignified farewell in peace and quiet". Pidurutalagala is the highest mountain in Sri Lanka, although at only a little over 2,500 metres, it was smaller than most of the Alps that Hesse was used to back in his native Germany and Switzerland.

Hesse was determined to view the landscape of the East without sentimental mysticism or what we would now call "orientalism". As he climbed alone in the coolness of a rainy morning, he noted that the cool green mountain valley of Nuwara Eliya was silvery in the light morning rain. Passing the typically Anglo-Indian tea plantations with their corrugated tin roofs, there was a marked difference between the extravagantly extensive tennis courts and golf links for the owners, and the Singhalese workers who sat shivering in woollen shawls in front of their huts as they deloused themselves.

The landscape reminded him oddly of the Black Forest, and at that time in the early morning he described it as being "lifeless and shrouded: except for a few birds I saw no signs of life until, in a garden hedge, I came upon a fat, poison-green chameleon whose malevolent movements in snatching insects I observed for some time."

But when he reached the summit, he received what he described as:

The grandest and purest impression I took away from all Ceylon. The wind had just swept clean the whole long valley of Nuwara Eliya, I saw, deep blue and immense, the entire high mountain system of Ceylon piled up in mighty walls, and in its midst the beautiful, ancient, and holy pyramid of Adam's Peak. Beside it

at an infinite depth and distance lay flat blue sea, in between a thousand mountains, broad valleys, narrow ravines, rivers and waterfalls, in countless folds, the whole mountainous island on which ancient legends placed paradise.

Up until then, Hesse felt he had found it impossible to assimilate the difference of the East; that he was searching more for some way of resolving what he described as "his own divided self", and that it was impossible not to remain "a stranger without citizenship" in such a country.

But on the summit of this mountain, he had what can only be described as an epiphany, when he felt that for the first time the primeval landscape "spoke to him": "Only up here in the cold air and the seething clouds of the raw heights did it become fully clear to me how completely our being and our northern culture are rooted in raw, impoverished lands."

There were other notable descriptions of Sri Lanka at around this time – notably Leonard Woolf's first novel, *The Village in the Jungle*, published in the same year, 1913, as Herman Hesse's *Aus Indien* – but it is hard to beat Hesse for the way he penetrated to the heart of what he saw as Sri Lanka's complicated mystery.

Opposite: "The entrance to a temple in Ceylon". Photograph by E. B. Gibbes, 1910.

Above: "Map of the Island of Ceylon", by A. M. Ferguson, 1875, detail showing Central Province. The old kingdom of Kandy still had a mystique about it.

Following pages: "Adam's Peak falls in Ceylon". Photograph by B. F. K. Rives, 1880-85. When Hesse went up to the summit of Pidurutalagala, he saw "deep blue and immense, the entire high mountain system of Ceylon piled up in mighty walls, and in its midst the beautiful, ancient, and holy pyramid of Adam's Peak" (*Aus Indien*, 1913).

Around the World on a Bicycle

Get a bicycle. You will not regret it. If you live.

(Mark Twain, "Taming the Bicycle", 1917)

A startling invention of the nineteenth century brought a whole new wave of maps. The invention of the "ordinary" or "penny-farthing" bicycle with its tensioned wheel in 1869 allowed for a completely different way of travelling.

Not that they were necessarily easy machines to master. They were nicknamed "penny-farthings" because of their disproportionate wheels: the very large front one (the "penny") compared to the much smaller rear one (the "farthing").

Because the seat was high off the ground, mounting required considerable skill. The intrepid rider had to grasp the handlebar and place one foot on a peg above the back wheel, then push forward to gain momentum and nimbly jump up onto the seat and balance while moving. That at least was the theory. Mark Twain, in his amusing essay "Taming the Bicycle", described the equal difficulties of getting off one: "It sounds exceedingly easy; but it isn't. I don't know why it isn't, but it isn't. Try as you may, you don't get down as you would from a horse, you get down as you would from a house afire. You make a spectacle of yourself every time."

Right: "Thomas Stevens". Illustration from *Around the World on a Bicycle* by Thomas Stevens, 1887–88. Sporting, appropriately enough, a handlebar moustache, he made a dashing figure as an ambassador for cycling.

Opposite: "S. L. Johnson's New Tourist & Cyclists Road Map, to & from London, Croydon, Epsom, Redhill, Reigate, Tunbridge Wells, Brighton, Hastings, Lewes and Eastbourne", *c*.1894.

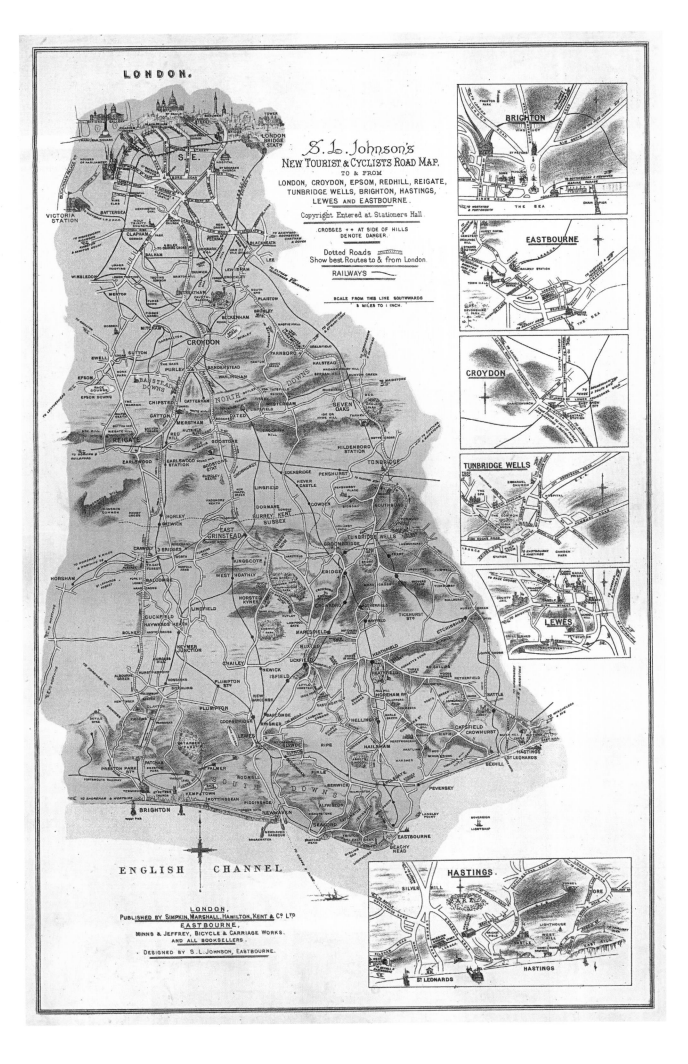

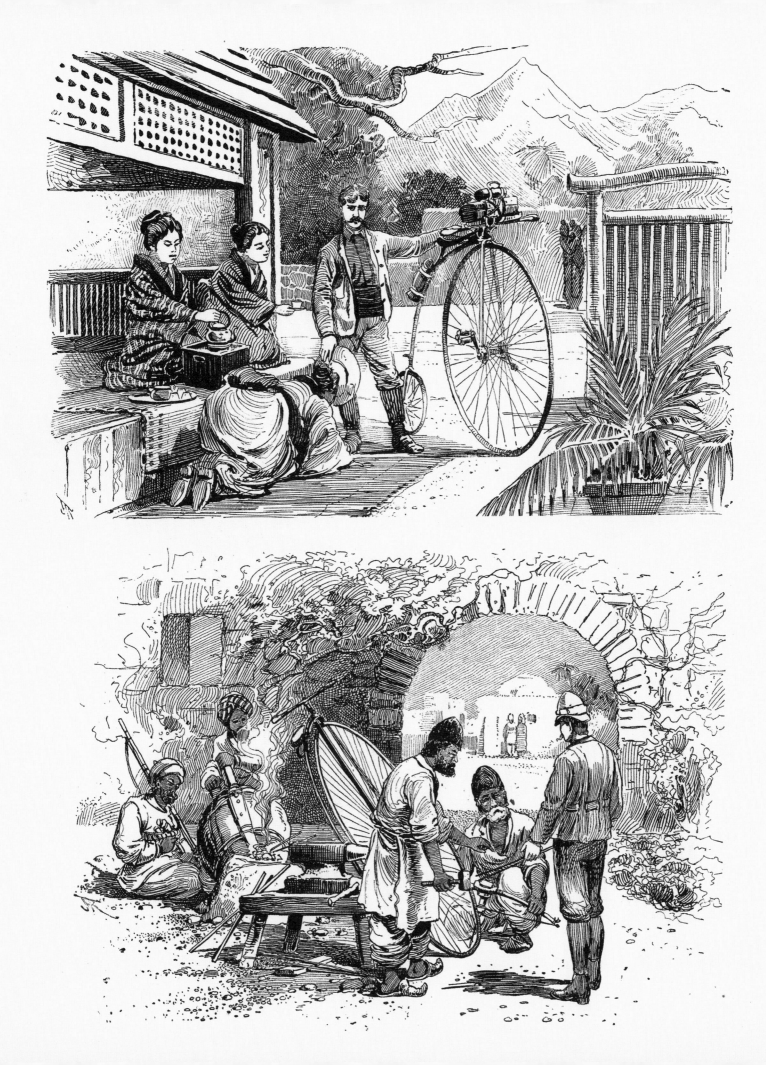

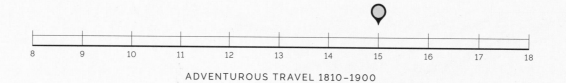

Above, left: "The start". Illustration from *Around the World on a Bicycle* by Thomas Stevens, 1887–88.

Above, right: "We reach Chalakua". Illustration from *Around the World on a Bicycle* by Thomas Stevens, 1887–88. His journey from San Francisco around the world took him two and a half years.

Left: "Wantonly assaulted". Illustration from *Around the World on a Bicycle* by Thomas Stevens, 1887–88.

Opposite: "The Champs Elysée at 10 pm". Illustration from *Around the World on a Bicycle* by Thomas Stevens, 1887–88.

W.A.Rogers

the prototype of the new "safety" bicycle appeared, with a strong diamond frame and pneumatic tyres. It was so clearly superior to the "ordinary" bicycle, as penny-farthings had been called, that they soon became a rarity. Cyclists appreciated a bicycle where you could put your feet down on either side to stop and were unlikely to do a header over the handle bars. A women's model of the "safety" bicycle proved particularly successful.

The maps that accompanied this cycling revolution were often streamlined of all extraneous detail. From the earliest days to the modern lycra-clad warrior of the velodrome, cyclists have never liked to carry excess weight (Stevens survived with minimal clothing and had all his maps sent out to him by relay). The "Cyclists' Road Map" of 1894 (p.137) shows the lanes connecting the South and North Downs, which then as now have always been attractive to cyclists on day trips from London. Perhaps if some of them managed to reach Brighton, they may have been inspired to emulate Stevens and cross the Channel to France, Europe and indeed the world.

Making the Planet a Smaller Place

"I will bet twenty thousand pounds against anyone who wishes that I will make the tour of the world in eighty days or less; in nineteen hundred and twenty hours, or a hundred and fifteen thousand two hundred minutes. Do you accept?"

"We accept," replied Messrs. Stuart, Fallentin, Sullivan, Flanagan, and Ralph, after consulting each other.

"Good," said Mr. Fogg. "The train leaves for Dover at a quarter before nine. I will take it."

(Jules Verne, *Around the World in Eighty Days*, 1873)

By the second half of the nineteenth century, technological innovations were rapidly making the world a smaller place for travellers. Then in just two years, 1869 and 1870, some breakthroughs accelerated this progress and made a really fast circumnavigation of the planet possible. The first Transcontinental Railroad was completed in America in 1869, and in 1870 the Suez Canal opened, as did a completed Indian railway system across the subcontinent.

It is when Phileas Fogg reads an account of this last development in the *Daily Telegraph* in his club, the Reform, that he proposes to make such a circumnavigation in less than 80 days to his fellow whist players – and is prepared to stake a considerable part of his fortune as a bet to do so, just to give narrative edge to the proceedings.

Jules Verne's book was published in 1873 and was a resounding success. It appealed to the mood of the times, and has caught the imagination of filmmakers and travellers like Michael Palin ever since.

Opposite: "Suez Canal". Photographer unknown, *c.*1890. The opening of the Suez Canal in 1870, along with the completion of the Transcontinental Railroad in America in 1869, and the Indian railway system across the subcontinent, meant that a fast passage around the world was suddenly possible.

Above: "Central Pacific Railroad train and coaches in Yosemite Valley". Photograph by Carleton Watkins, 1861–69.

Following pages: "Isochronic Passage Chart for Travellers, showing the shortest number of days journey from London by the quickest through routes and using such further conveyances as are available without unreasonable cost. It is supposed that local preparations have been made and that other circumstances are favorable". By Francis Galton, F.R.S. Published for the *Proceedings of the Royal Geographical Society*, 1881.

ISOCHRONIC PASSAGE CHART
FOR TRAVELLERS,

showing the shortest number of days journey
from London by the quickest through routes
and using such further conveyances as are
available without unreasonable cost.   It is
supposed that local preparations have been
made and that other circumstances are favorable.

By Francis Galton. F.R.S.

H. Sharbau. R.G.S. del.

Explanation of colours.   Green ▨ within 10 days.   Yellow ▭ 10–20 days.   Pi

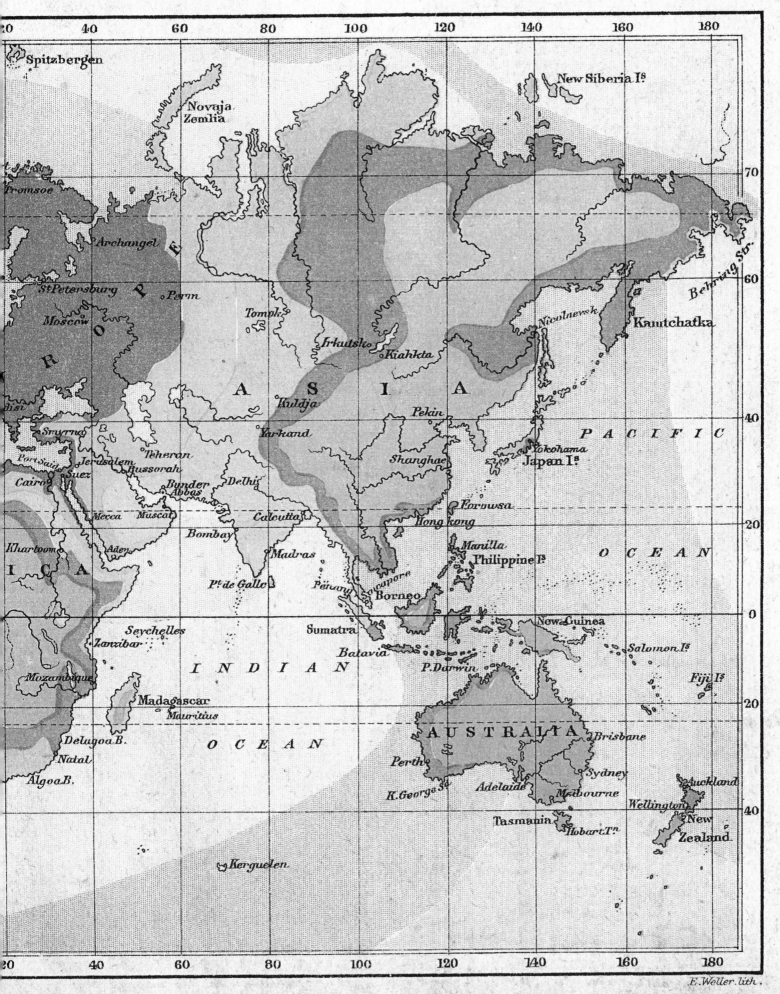

Spitzbergen
Novaja Zemlia
New Siberia Is
Tromsoe
Archangel
St Petersburg
Peron
Moscow
Tompk.
Irkutsko
Nicolaevsk
Kamtchatka
Kiahkta
EUROPE
ASIA
Kuldja
Smyrna
Teheran
Pekin
PACIFIC
Jerusalem
Bussorah
Yarkand
Port Said
Bunder
Delhi
Shanghae
Yokohama
Cairo
Suez
Abbas
Japan Is
Khartoom
Mecca
Muscat
Calcutta
Formosa
AFRICA
Bombay
Hong kong
Aden
OCEAN
Madras
Manilla
Philippine Is
Pt de Gallo
Penang
Seychelles
Sumatra
Singapore
Borneo
New Guinea
Salomon Is
Zanzibar
INDIAN
Batavia
P. Darwin
Fiji Is
Mozambique
Madagascar
AUSTRALIA
Brisbane
Mauritius
Delagoa B.
OCEAN
Perth
Sydney
Natal
K. George Sd
Adelaide
Auckland
Algoa B.
Melbourne
Wellington
Tasmania
New
Hobart Tn
Zealand
Kerguelen

E. Weller. lith.

20-30 days. Blue ▮▮▮ 30-40 days. Brown ▮▮▮ more than 40 days journey.

The first around-the-world journey for tourists had already been organized by that travel impresario of the nineteenth century, Thomas Cook. It left in September 1872 and returned seven months later. Drawing on a series of travellers' letters, an account was published in 1873 as *Letters from the Sea and from Foreign Lands, Descriptive of a Tour Around the World*.

Some have argued that Jules Verne drew on this for his own work, although this seems unlikely given the proximity of publication dates; he may, however, have been aware that a tour was happening. What is more certain is that as an idea it was current and "in the air". Verne even went so far as to include in his novel the chart produced by the *Daily Telegraph* after the Great Indian Peninsula Railway was completed, showing that a circumnavigation of 80 days was possible.

Above: Jules Verne. "It was as if he wanted a travel novel to end all travel novels."

Opposite: "A double loop on Darjeeling Hill Railway, West Bengal, East India". Photograph by Johnston & Hoffman, 1880–90.

Around The World In Eighty Days was the most commercially successful of Verne's novels. It remains an endlessly attractive concept, with the bet his friends at the Reform Club in London make that Phileas Fogg can't complete the journey in time; the contrast between Fogg's phlegmatic English gentleman and his servant Passepartout's excitable Frenchman; and the schoolboy pleasure that comes from the twist at the end. For although it takes him 81 days to complete the journey, because he travels from west to east, he crosses the dateline and therefore gains a day in the process, so wins the wager.

Given Verne had never travelled east of Europe, he had to use considerable amounts of imagination in his description of some of the more exotic places on Phileas Fogg's itinerary. He drew many from encyclopaedias and the very same *Bradshaw's Guide* that Fogg carries with him. This is his description of the Andaman Islands when Fogg and Passepartout first see them:

Opposite: The cover of Jules Verne's *Around the World in Eighty Days* (1873), one of his greatest successes that captured the popular imagination.

Right: "Sir Francis Galton (1822–1911)". The Victorian polymath who produced this map did everything from devising a method for classifying fingerprints to inventing a whistle for assessing hearing ability.

Following pages: "Isochronic Distances" from *An Atlas of Economic Geography* by J. G. Bartholomew, 1914. An isochronic map is one devised to show how long it would take to reach any given part of the world from a set starting point.

> *The panorama presented by these islands was superb. The foreground was a mass of forests and fan palms, areca, bamboo, nutmeg, teak, gigantic mimosa and arborescent ferns, and behind this maze of greenery the mountains rose in graceful outlines against the sky. Along the coast swarmed in their thousands the precious swallows, whose edible nests are esteemed a great delicacy in this Celestial Empire.*

One irony of the success of *Around The World In Eighty Days* was that it enabled Jules Verne to travel widely himself for the first time. And how did he choose to travel? By taking cruises in his newly acquired yacht.

When Verne published the book in 1873, he had already written *Journey to the Centre of the Earth* (1864); *From the Earth to the Moon* (1865) and *Twenty Thousand Leagues Under the Sea* (1869), on top of a host of other "*Voyages Extraordinaires*" by balloon, sea or land, across Africa or to the North Pole.

It was as if he wanted a travel novel to end all travel novels – one that truly circumnavigated the globe and trumped any other, including his own previous ones. And it came out of the very nineteenth-century sense that with technological advancement – and Verne was forever fascinated by technology – the world was now a smaller place; a known, explored and discovered place, with no secrets left. As long as one knew the timetable, one could, like Phileas Fogg, travel around it with ease.

This map (see pp.146–47) at the start of the following decade, in 1881, is by a talented and eccentric Fellow of the Royal Geographical Society who rivalled Verne in the extraordinarily wide range of his interests. Sir Francis Galton was a Victorian polymath who did everything from devising a method for classifying fingerprints to inventing a whistle for assessing hearing ability; he studied statistics, eugenics – a term he invented – and the optimal method for making tea.

He also travelled widely – far more so than Verne – which is perhaps why he became interested in doing this isochronic chart, a map devised to show how many days it would take to reach any given part of the world. He is careful to make the disclaimer, just as Phileas Fogg does in the novel, that "it is supposed that local preparations have been made and that other circumstances are favourable."

The map, whether by accident or design, emulates one feature of Jules Verne's novel. For if the furthest place on earth can be reached in 40 days, as Galton proposes, then it stands to reason that it can only take 40 days to return back to England, so 80 in total. Perhaps Galton was minded, as Fogg had been, to propose a bet with the other Fellows of the Royal Geographical Society and have them waiting for him in the lecture hall on his return.

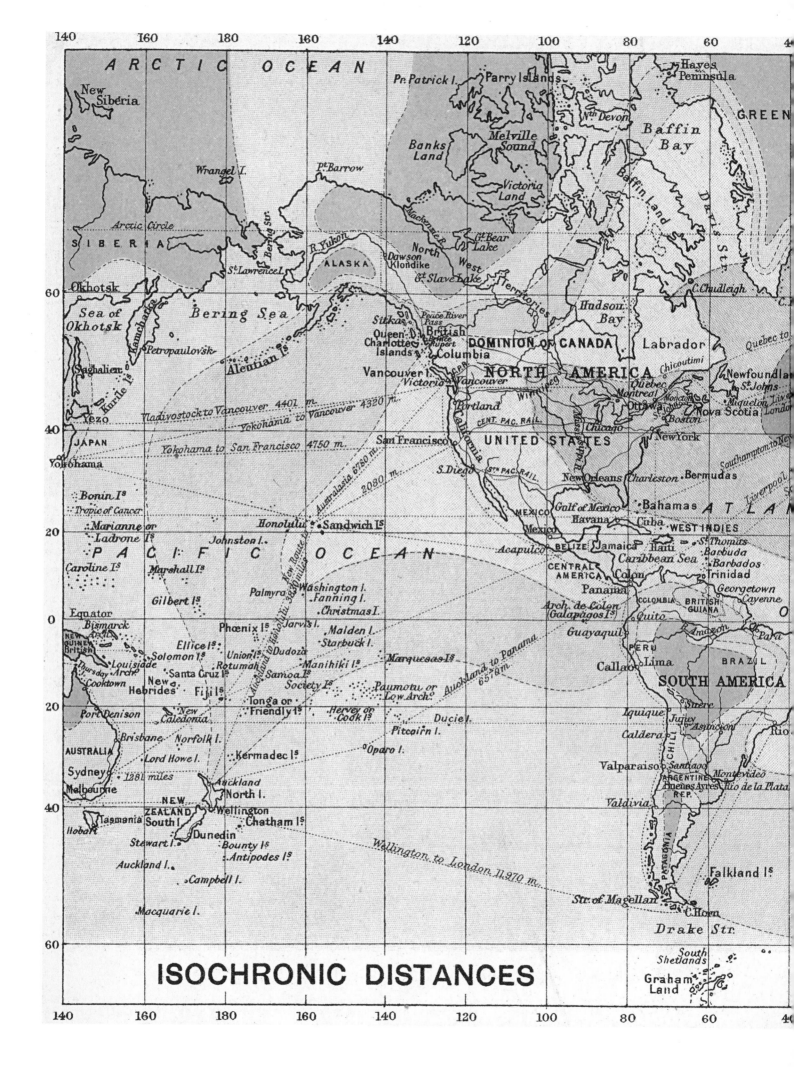

ISOCHRONIC DISTANCES

DISTANCES IN DAYS FROM LONDON

| in 5 days journey | 5 to 10 days | 10 to 20 days | 20 to 30 days | 30 to 40 days | Over 40 days |

Through Persia on a Mule

I know now pretty well what to expect in Persia: not to look for surprises of beauty and luxuriance, and to be satisfied with occasional oases of cultivation among brown, rocky, treeless hills, varied by brown villages with crops and spindly poplars and willows, contrasting with the harsh barrenness of the surrounding gravelly waste.

(Isabella Bird, *Journeys in Persia and Kurdistan*, 1891)

Isabella Bird (1831–1904) was one of the most impressive travellers of the late nineteenth century.

She had been brought up in sheltered and conventional Victorian conditions, the daughter of a clergyman. For her young adult life, she followed the expectations of the time and pursued charitable causes at home in Scotland. The effects of this constraint were to make her ill, both physically and psychologically. She suffered from disabling depressions, headaches and even spinal disease.

All these dropped away from her when, in 1872 at the age of 41, she made a startling decision. She decided to sail to the other side of the world for Hawaii (then called the Sandwich Isles) and begin a new life of adventurous travel. By the time she had climbed the 17,000-foot high Mauna Loa, one of the largest volcanoes on the planet, she was already demonstrating the qualities that led one of her early biographers to comment:

As a traveller Mrs. Bishop [as Isabella Bird was known under her married name] has the outstanding merit that she nearly always conquered her territories alone; that she faced the wilderness almost single-handed; that she observed and recorded without companionship. She suffered no toil

to impede her, no study to repel her. She triumphed over her own limitations of health and strength as over the dangers of the road.

(Anna M. Stoddart, *The Life of Isabella Bird (Mrs Bishop)*, 1906)

More was to follow. She set off for Colorado, where she lived an equally adventurous life and wrote what became one of the travel bestsellers of its day, *A Lady's Life in the Rocky Mountains*, with its discreet hints of romance with an outlaw desperado called Jim Nugent.

Her work on Persia relates to a later period in 1890 when Isabella, now almost 60 and widowed after a brief marriage, decided both courageously and typically to make a journey across that country.

Just getting there proved difficult. She spent some time in India trying to arrange a passage there (although typically she made an adventurous diversion to Ladakh on a yak to prevent her from becoming bored). She then met a younger army officer called Major Sawyer who to all intents and purposes was a spy and may have felt that Isabella would provide him with good cover for his own journey to Persia.

Opposite: "Kurd girls". Photograph by P. M. Sykes, 1901. Bird was dismayed by the treatment she witnessed of women.

PERSIA
AFGHANISTAN
AND BALUCHISTÁN

Sketch Map to illustrate the journeys of

MAJOR P. M. SYKES
(Queen's Bays)

H.M's Consul, Kermán & Persian Baluchistán.

Scale of Miles

Nat Scale 1:5000000 or 79 miles = 1 inch.

Reference to Routes.

1st Journey Jan to June 1893.

2nd   Oct.1893 to June 1894.

3rd   Dec.1894 to Mar.1897.

4th   Nov.1897 to Jan.1901.

Route of Alexander the Great

Marco Polo

Railways   Heights in feet.

Published by the Royal Geographical Society.

One of the great strengths of Isabella's writing is that she never succumbs to orientalism; she casts a cold eye on the realities of Persian life and indeed of the travelling experience.

Deciding to ride a saddle mule (she usually stuck to horses and found the mule uncomfortable), she engaged a team of muleteers and set off with her revolver, accompanied by Major Sawyer, for what she afterwards described as an "awful journey".

I never would have undertaken it had I known the hardships it would involve, the long marches, the wretched food, the abominable accommodation, the filthy water, the brutal barbarism of the people ... We have been marching day after day from eighteen to twenty-two miles with mercury at from four to twelve degrees below the zero of Fahrenheit, through snow from 18 in. to 3 ft. deep, sometimes getting on at only one and a half miles an hour, and putting up at night either in cold, filthy, and horrible caravanserais with three or four hundred mules and their drivers or in Kurdish houses shared with mules, asses, cows, and sheep.

(Isabella Bird, *Journeys in Persia and Kurdistan*, 1890)

A sharp observer of the political realities she encountered, she described the Persia she found as "a ruined, played-out country, perishing for want of people, of water, of fuel, and above all for want of security, crushed by the most grinding exactions to which there is no limit but the total ruin of those on whom they press, without a middle class and without hope."

She was particularly dismayed by the treatment of women: "They have nothing to do and see no one. If a woman of the poorer class has occasion to go out to get food, she puts on a black mask and a large blue sheet, which covers her from head to foot. Any woman going out otherwise would be put to death." She herself was often "hooted, spat upon, and howled at by a rabble of fanatical men and boys".

By the time she got to Teheran some of the muleteers had died when they were caught in a particularly severe snowstorm crossing the Sona pass. Isabella herself had lost 32 lbs in weight after the 46 days of their journey from Baghdad.

Undeterred, she pressed on to Isfahan where, "refitting my dear old tent with new ropes", she ventured into the nomadic

Left: "Persia, Afghanistan and Baluchistan, sketch map to illustrate the journeys of Major P. M. Sykes". Royal Geographical Society, 1902.

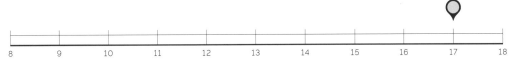

Opposite: "Zard Kuh range". Illustration from *Journeys in Persia and Kurdistan* by Mrs Bishop (Isabella L. Bird), 1891. "I never would have undertaken the awful journey had I known the hardships it would involve, the long marches, the wretched food, the abominable accommodation, the filthy water, the brutal barbarism of the people…"

Above, top: "A Turkish Frontier Fort". Illustration from *Journeys in Persia and Kurdistan* by Mrs Bishop (Isabella L. Bird), 1891.

Left: "Mrs Bishop in her travelling dress at Erzeroum". Photograph from *The Life of Isabella Bird (Mrs Bishop)* by Anna M. Stoddart, 1906. One of the most impressive travellers of the late nineteenth century.

Right: "Mrs Bishop's tent on her ride amongst the Bakhtiari Lurs". Photograph from *The Life of Isabella Bird (Mrs Bishop)* by Anna M. Stoddart, 1906. At Isfahan she records "refitting my dear old tent with new ropes."

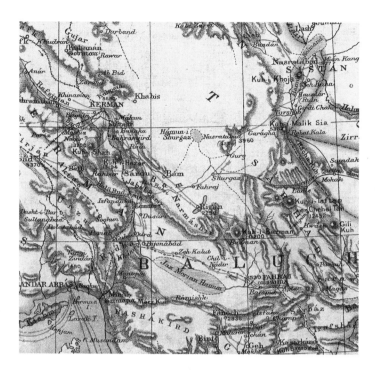

country of the Bakhtiari, before embarking on the equally hazardous route back through Kurdistan to Trebizond on the Black Sea coast. In all, she covered some 2,500 miles from Baghdad through Persia and Armenia.

When *Journeys in Persia and Kurdistan* first appeared, to critical if not commercial success, some reviewers expressed surprise that "a member of the weaker sex" should have managed such an extraordinary journey.

This fine map (see pp.156–57) from the collection of the Royal Geographical Society was made just a few years later to illustrate the journeys of Major Percy Sykes, another early reconnaissance spy who also made extensive journeys around Persia, as evidenced by the elegant tracery of red lines showing his routes. His sister, Ella C. Sykes, who shared many of her brother's travels, produced a book, *Through Persia on a Sidesaddle*; Sykes himself went on later to command British troops in Persia during the First World War.

Above: "Persia, Afghanistan and Baluchistan, sketch map to illustrate the journeys of Major P. M. Sykes". Royal Geographical Society, 1902, detail. "A wild and mountainous country for any traveller to cross."

Right: "Fording the Karun". Illustration from *Journeys in Persia and Kurdistan* by Mrs Bishop (Isabella L. Bird), 1891.

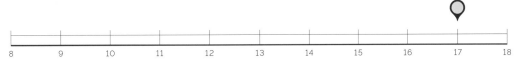

India's Summer Capital of Pleasure

This wonderful map (see pp.164–65) is a fascinating by-product of The Great Trigonometrical Survey of India, one of the most extensive cartographic endeavours ever undertaken. It is a detailed examination of Mussoorie, the hill station where the most famous director of that survey – and the man who gave his name to the highest mountain in the world – George Everest once lived.

The Great Trigonometrical Survey of India was begun in 1802 by the East India Company as an ambitious project to measure the entire subcontinent with scientific precision. It was originally hoped the project would take only five years, but so demanding was the task and so varied the terrain that it was to be another 70 years (well after the company's rule in India had come to an end) before the epic task was finished.

The survey began in 1802 in the far south of India with the measurement of a baseline near Madras. By 1823, George Everest had become superintendent and it was he who was responsible for surveying the meridian arc from the southernmost point of India north to Nepal, a distance of about 1,500 miles. He was made Surveyor General of India in 1830, before retiring in 1843 and returning to England; by that time he was not a well man, as the effects of fever and rheumatism had left him half paralyzed and he had earlier experienced the debilitating effects of malaria.

However in 1865, long after Everest had come back to England, the Royal Geographical Society renamed Peak XV in Nepal – at the time only recently identified as the world's highest peak – after him. His successor as Surveyor General, Andrew Scott Waugh, who was considered Everest's protégé and was indebted to Everest for his own appointment, suggested this without a blush. Everest himself demurred at the honour, as he

Above: "Lambton's Great Theodolite used by William Lambton and George Everest during the Great Trigonometrical Survey of India". Photographer unknown, 1830–45.

Opposite: "Index Chart to the Great Trigonometrical Survey of India", 1885.

Following pages: "Guide Map for Mussoorie and Landour, Prepared from the Large Scale Maps of the Great Trigonometrical Survey of India", 1871.

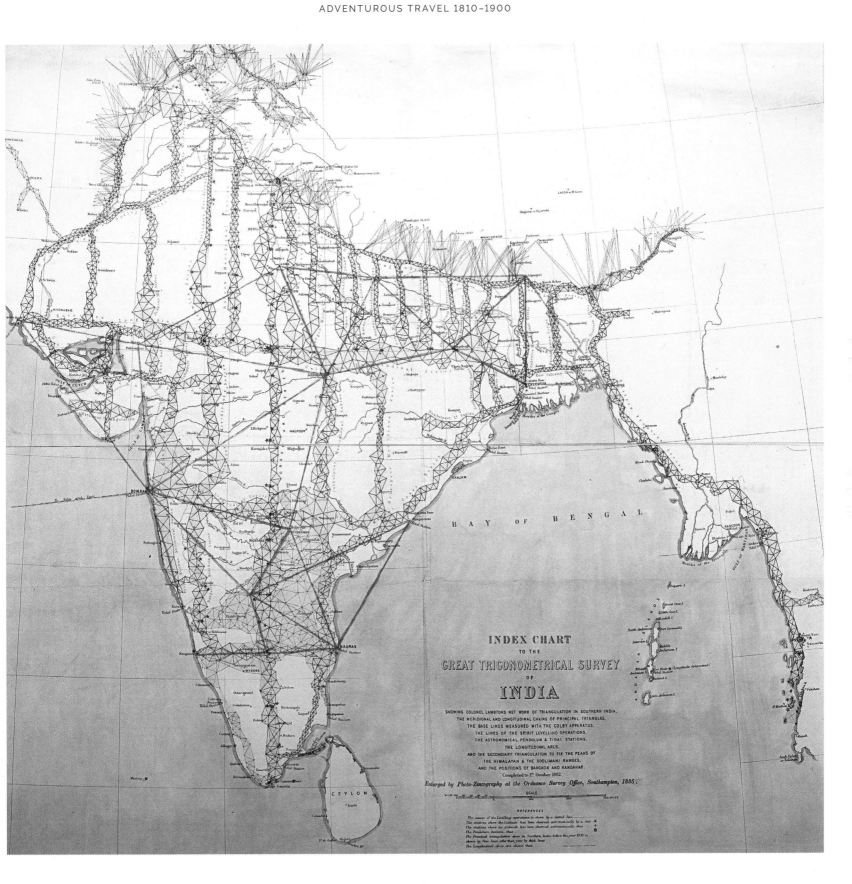

INDEX CHART
TO THE
GREAT TRIGONOMETRICAL SURVEY
OF
INDIA

SHOWING COLONEL LAMBTON'S NET WORK OF TRIANGULATION IN SOUTHERN INDIA,
THE MERIDIONAL AND LONGITUDINAL CHAINS OF PRINCIPAL TRIANGLES,
THE BASE LINES MEASURED WITH THE COLBY APPARATUS,
THE LINES OF THE SPIRIT LEVELLING OPERATIONS,
THE ASTRONOMICAL, PENDULUM & TIDAL STATIONS,
THE LONGITUDINAL ARCS,
AND THE SECONDARY TRIANGULATION TO FIX THE PEAKS OF
THE HIMALAYAN & THE SOOLIMANI RANGES,
AND THE POSITIONS OF BANGKOK AND KANDAHAR.
Completed to 1st October 1882.

Enlarged by Photo-Zincography at the Ordnance Survey Office, Southampton, 1885.

SCALE

REFERENCES

BAY OF BENGAL

CEYLON

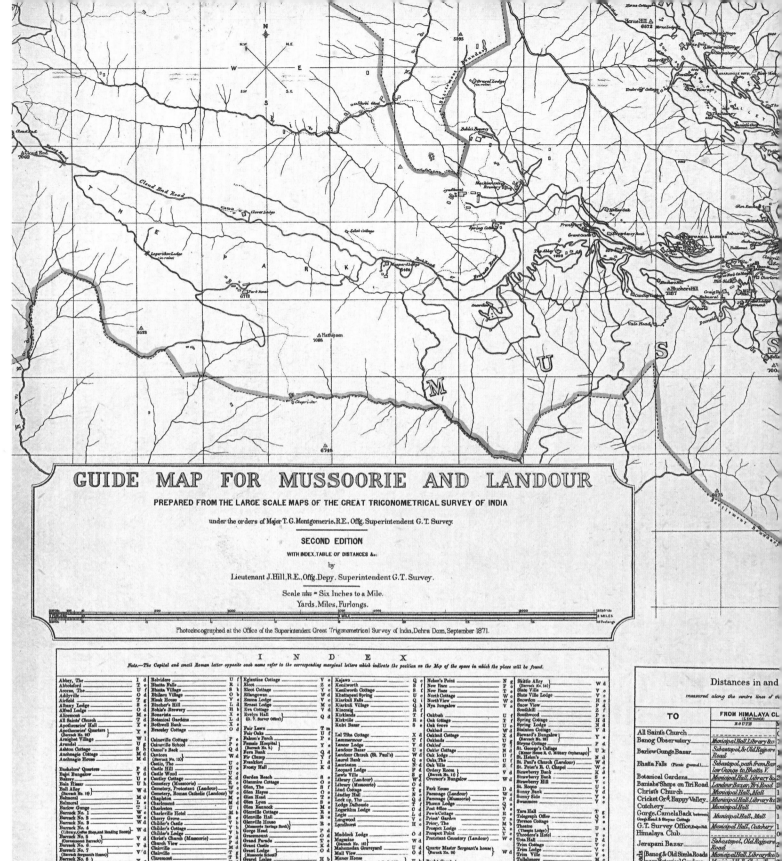

GUIDE MAP FOR MUSSOORIE AND LANDOUR

PREPARED FROM THE LARGE SCALE MAPS OF THE GREAT TRIGONOMETRICAL SURVEY OF INDIA

under the orders of Major T. G. Montgomerie, R.E., Offg. Superintendent G.T. Survey.

SECOND EDITION

WITH INDEX, TABLE OF DISTANCES &c.

by

Lieutenant J. Hill, R.E., Offg. Depy. Superintendent G.T. Survey.

Scale = Six Inches to a Mile.

Yards, Miles, Furlongs.

Photozincographed at the Office of the Superintendent Great Trigonometrical Survey of India, Dehra Doon, September 1871.

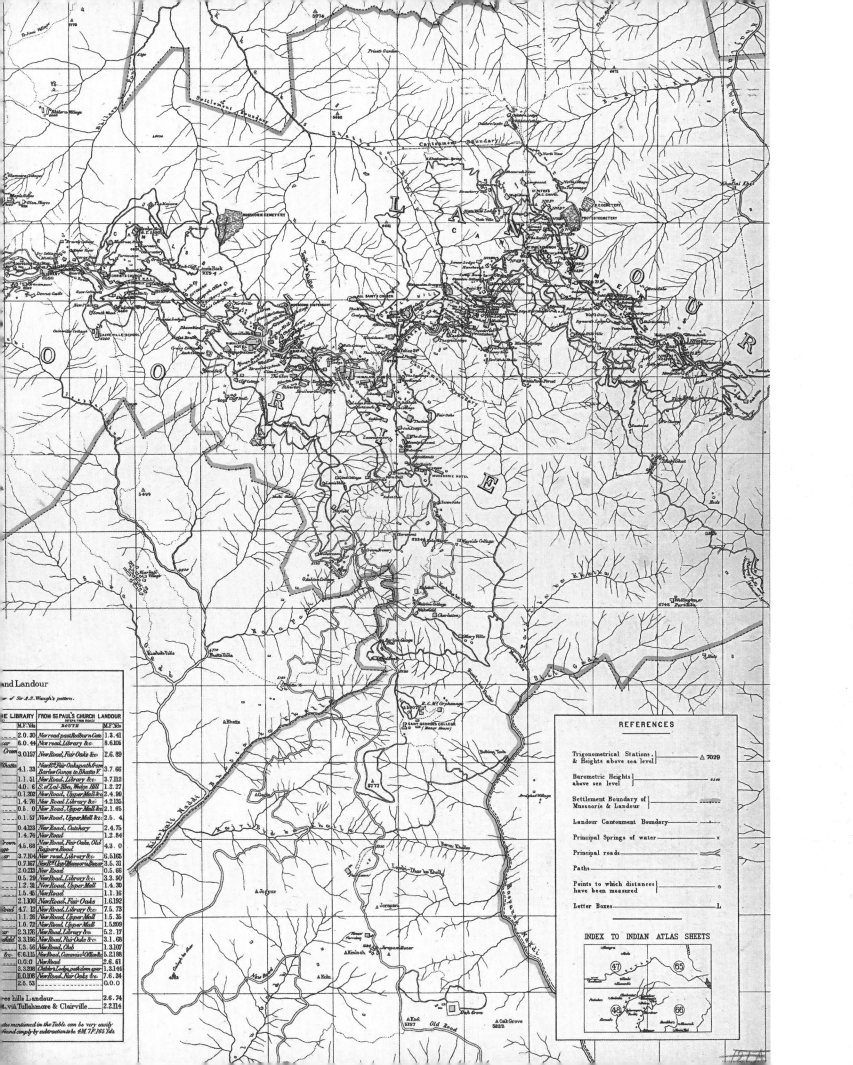

Above: "Mussoorie". Photograph by Colonel Sir Thomas H. Holdich, 1917. Mussoorie became India's "summer capital of pleasure".

Opposite: "Portrait of Sir George Everest (1790–1866), Surveyor General of India from 1830 to 1843". Photograph by Maull & Polyblank. The Surveyor General of India never saw the mountain that bears his name.

had never even seen the mountain – and pointed out, moreover, that his name was not easily written or pronounced in Hindi.

But George Everest did have a strong association with the high Himalaya. For many years when he was in India, he had lived at Park House in Mussoorie (the house can be seen to the far west of the town on this map with, appropriately enough, Everest Road leading to it). Mussoorie was a hill station north of Delhi with a convenient position, as it was close to the Ganges and so the tributaries of that great river could be followed up into the Himalaya by the surveyors for the Great Trigonometrical Survey. Indeed for many years the survey had its offices in the nearby, more low-lying, town of Dehra Dun.

Mussoorie had originally been founded early in the nineteenth century by a young and enterprising lieutenant called Frederick Young, who had hunted in the area and appreciated its cool climate in the spring when the plains of Delhi were becoming unbearable. For just that reason, it soon became famous as a hill station to which government *sahibs* and their *memsahibs* could retreat.

The writer Bill Aitken, who has long lived in Mussoorie, commented that:

> *... there is an irony in the British Empire's assumption that they invented the idea of hill stations where they could "aestivate and cut the summer heat" – when, in actual fact, it was the Hindu gods who started this notion of wintering in the lower regions and spending the summer in the snowy heights. Long before the Alpine Club was founded, the Hindu gods – and goddesses – had cottoned on to the idea that the mountains were a wonderful place to be in hot weather.*

Mussoorie always had a subtly different atmosphere from its more famous rival hill station of Simla. While Simla attracted senior and respectable members of the colonial government – in 1864, it was formally declared "the summer capital of British India" – Mussoorie had a wilder, more deracinated reputation. In some ways it could be said that Mussoorie became India's "summer capital of pleasure."

The Himalaya Hotel (later renamed the Savoy) was a centre for that entertainment right through the nineteenth and into the twentieth century. Queen Mary stayed there and sent a carved Indian walking-stick back to Edward VII. In the 1920s, the ballroom was still constantly full, as the Raj danced out its small hours in a riot of high society and frenzied high-altitude adultery.

One contemporary guest recorded that "when the morning bell sounded, the pious would say their prayers while the impious get back into their own beds." As Rudyard Kipling wrote:

> *I had a little husband*
> *Who gave me all his pay,*
> *I left him for Mussoorie*
> *A hundred miles away.*
> *I dragged my little husband's name*
> *Through heaps of social mire,*
> *And joined him in October*
> *As good as you'd desire.*

It is not surprising that this lavish walking map (see pp.164–65) should have been produced at the luxurious scale of six inches to the mile, so that visiting sahibs could promenade along the walkways and admire the distant views of the Himalaya. Some did more than just admire. Members of the Alpine Club attempted to reach nearby Nanda Devi with what soon became obsessive dedication and for one simple reason: at 25,640 feet high, it was not only the highest mountain in India, but the highest mountain in the whole of the British Empire. They failed in the attempt.

This area of the Southern Himalaya is filled with luxurious forests, and respect for trees has always run deep in the local Garhwali psyche. Giant deodars were often planted near Hindu temples, just as they now were by the British outside the Himalaya Hotel, where they can still be seen. Those doing any of the circuits from the Himalaya Club advised on this map, carefully calibrated to be not more than three miles in length so as not to exhaust any delicate British physiques in the sun, would have had the most spectacular views of what tradition in India had always held to be "the abode of the gods".

Opposite: "Nanda Devi from 20,000 ft on Nanda Kot". Photograph by T. G. Longstaff, 1905. Members of the Alpine Club attempted to reach nearby Nanda Devi with what soon became obsessive dedication and for one simple reason: at 25,640 feet high, it was not only the highest mountain in India, but the highest mountain in the whole of the British Empire.

Above: "Himalayas near Mussoorie". Watercolour by Colonel Sir Thomas H. Holdich, 1880s. This area of the Southern Himalaya is filled with luxurious forests and spectacular views.

Personal Travel

1900–1970

Right: "Nouveau Paris Monumental: Itineraire Pratique de l'Étranger dans Paris", 1907.

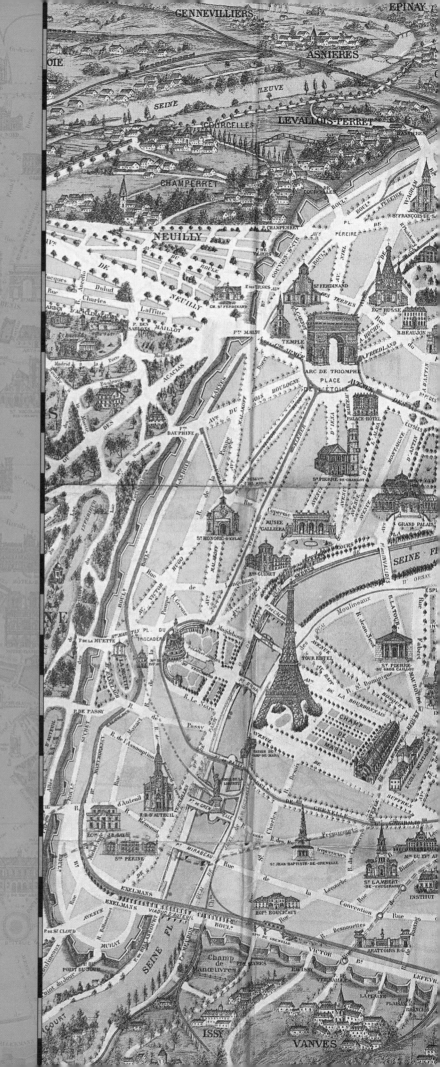

Go and Look Beyond the Ranges

When this Bartholomew's Map was published in 1912, South America was beginning to open up as a continent for travellers. The man who was to promote more tourism to the continent than perhaps anyone else in the twentieth century, Hiram Bingham, had just made a momentous discovery.

One could say that Hiram Bingham was a man who needed to become famous. Born in 1875, he had grown up in Hawaii, the son of a missionary family who had once been celebrated and prosperous but had descended into genteel poverty. As Hiram Bingham III, he was conscious both of his ancestor's fame (the first Hiram Bingham had almost single-handedly converted the islands to Christianity) and of the family's fall from grace.

In *Lost City of the Incas* (1948), he fondly remembers climbing "a number of mountains in the suburbs of Honolulu" as a boy

and often notes occasional and unexpected similarities between the Peruvian Vilcabamba and the green islands of Hawaii. The impression given is of a youth lived under open skies.

But in reality his childhood was a constrained one. He was cramped by a constant need for academic success and by the fierce religious fundamentalism of his parents, from which Bingham tried to escape. South America and Peru provided a freedom he had never had when young. As Che Guevara put it in an astute essay: "Machu Picchu was to Bingham the crowning of all his purest dreams as an adult child."

He was drawn early to the idea of South America, both because of its inherent romanticism and because in academic

Above: Hiram Bingham posing in the ruins of Machu Picchu.

Opposite: "Commercial Map of South America" by J. G. Bartholomew, 1912.

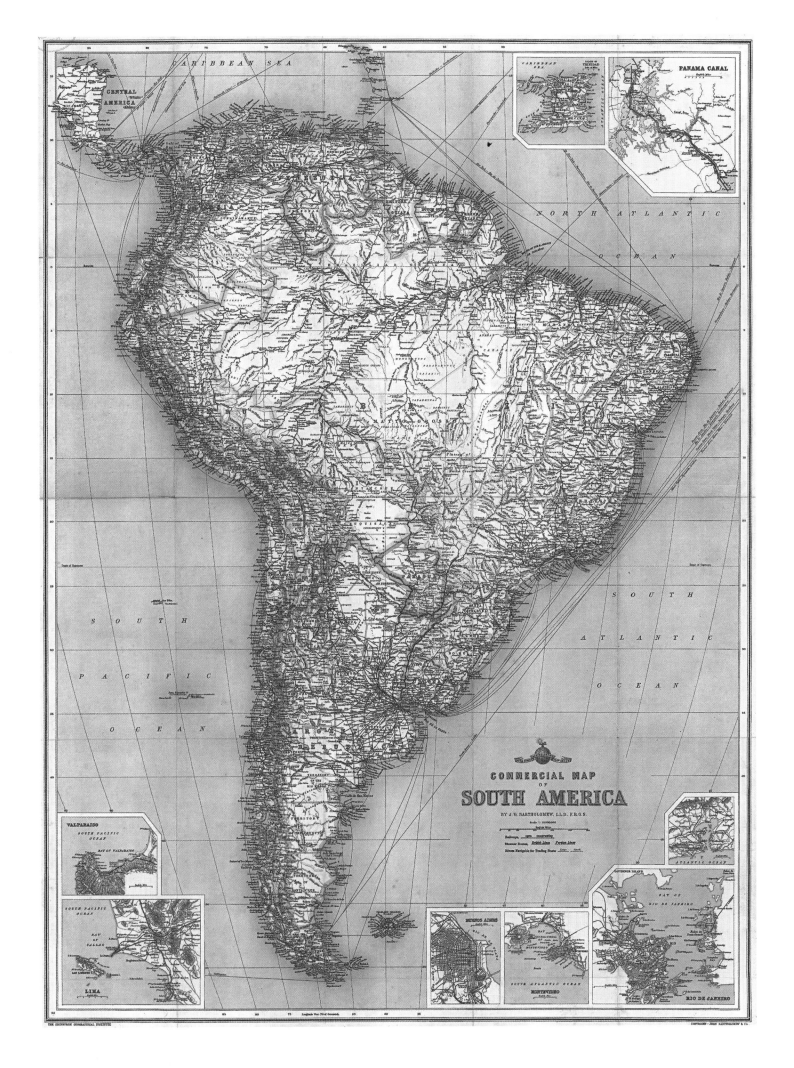

CARIBBEAN SEA

CENTRAL AMERICA

PANAMA CANAL

NORTH ATLANTIC OCEAN

SOUTH ATLANTIC OCEAN

SOUTH PACIFIC OCEAN

B R A Z I L

COMMERCIAL MAP
OF
SOUTH AMERICA

BY J. G. BARTHOLOMEW, LL.D., F.R.G.S.

Scale 1 : 18,000,000
English Miles

Railways, open .... constructing ....
Steamer Routes, British Lines .... Foreign Lines ....
Rivers Navigable for Trading Boats ....

VALPARAISO
SOUTH PACIFIC OCEAN
BAY OF VALPARAISO

SOUTH PACIFIC OCEAN
BAY OF CALLAO
LIMA

BUENOS AIRES
MONTEVIDEO
SOUTH ATLANTIC OCEAN

ATLANTIC OCEAN

BAY OF RIO DE JANEIRO
RIO DE JANEIRO

COPYRIGHT · JOHN BARTHOLOMEW & Co.

terms it was virgin territory. It was not yet a legitimate subject at the Ivy League universities and so Bingham could seize, as he put it, "the opportunity it presents to work in claims not already staked out". While Humboldt's books on South America in the early nineteenth century had instigated a wave of curiosity in Europe, and brought many travellers in his wake (particularly from France), North American interest in the southern continent had awoken more slowly. Only with the impressive histories of the Conquest of Mexico and Peru written later in the century by a Boston lawyer, William H. Prescott, had the process slowly begun.

Bingham managed to create a post for himself as Curator of the Harvard Library's non-existent "South American Collection", a collection that Bingham then set about creating. He quickly accumulated a card catalogue of some 25,000 items. When a consignment of Simón Bolívar's papers came his way, he decided, characteristically, to follow Bolívar's arduous route across South America to gauge how difficult it must have been for him and his men.

This was his first expedition, in 1906, when he was just 31. Despite or perhaps because of the hardships he encountered – his mules died and his local crewmen deserted them – it gave him a taste for exploration. He took a rifle, which he needed both for protection and to shoot game (he was later to issue a Winchester and a Colt to each member of his Peruvian teams). He published an account of it in his first book, *The Journal of an Expedition across Venezuela and Colombia* (1907).

Upon returning to the US, he became a Lecturer in South American history at his *alma mater*, Yale, a post that had been created especially for him and the first such post in any North American university. Bingham continued to press the case for more attention to be paid to his new subject in articles such as "The Possibilities of South American History and Politics as a Field for Research".

He was soon to head back to South America to do research himself, this time for a more ambitious expedition from Buenos Aires across the continent to Lima. With typical opportunism, Bingham managed to get appointed as the American delegate to a political conference in Chile, and he used this as a springboard for the trip. The resulting book, *Across South America* (1911), includes a chance encounter with Butch Cassidy and the Sundance Kid's gang – he ends up with one of their mules – as well as numerous other adventures. He was impressed, as is the map, by the scale of the Argentine railways which by then were carrying 30 million passengers a year. It also took him along the spine of the Andes, from Argentina up through Bolivia to the old Inca capital, Cusco.

As a result, he was accidentally propelled into a newfound subject, the Incas. Up until then, his focus had been on post-Columbian history, and while in Peru he wanted to visit Ayacucho, the scene of one of the climactic battles of Bolívar's Wars of Independence. To get there, he passed through the town of Abancay, where the Prefect persuaded him to join a treasure-hunting expedition he was mounting, doubtless because Bingham, as "an American professor", would give spurious legitimacy to the enterprise. The proposed destination was Choquequirao, the one Inca site in the Vilcabamba province that was already known, if little visited because of its difficult position high above the Apurímac river.

As Bingham cheerfully admits (his candour is one of the most attractive features of his writing), "we were not on the lookout for new Inca ruins and had never heard of Choquequirao." But he accepted the invitation with alacrity and,

Opposite, left: Hiram Bingham's expedition in the Andes.

Opposite, right: A tireless and energetic traveller, Hiram Bingham covered many thousands of miles in South America, often by mule.

Below: "Peru Central Railway, Ayacucho valley, 17,500ft". Photograph by W. S. Barclay, 1917.

despite the rigours of travelling there in the wet season, found his resulting experiences compelling.

Bingham's account of this in his most famous book, *Lost City of the Incas* (1948), ends with a famous clarion call to further exploration, inspired by the view from Choquequirao of the rest of the Vilcabamba range:

> *Those snow-capped peaks in an unknown and unexplored part of Peru fascinated me greatly. They tempted me to go and see what lay beyond. In the ever famous words of Rudyard Kipling there was "Something hidden! Go and find it! Go and look beyond the ranges – Something lost behind the ranges. Lost and waiting for you. Go!"*

Just a few years later in 1911, he did return, this time with a larger expedition. What was waiting for him beyond the ranges was the discovery of Machu Picchu, a discovery that put both Bingham and Peru on the map in a way that even he could never possibly have dreamed – and was to attract many millions of tourists to South America over the next century.

Above: "Street view, Cuzco". Photograph by J. W. Gregory, 1932.

Right: Hiram Bingham in front of his tent. One could say that Bingham was a man who needed to become famous.

Opposite: Machu Picchu before and after it had been cleared by Hiram Bingham in 1912.

The Monuments of Paris

Paris in the early twentieth century was a place of dynamic change which attracted a dizzying amount of visitors, drawn there by the city's artistic vitality. As Oscar Wilde quipped, "they say that when good Americans die, they go to Paris."

We have become so used to the Eiffel Tower, for instance, that we forget what it must have been like when it first appeared in 1889. It immediately became the world's tallest tower at over 1,000 feet, and remained so until the 1930s when the heavyweight Chrysler and Empire State Buildings arrived in New York to dispute that title. The Eiffel is still the tallest structure in Paris. No wonder it dominates the map of the city so much.

But there are two further and perhaps more surprising details about the Eiffel Tower. The first, given that it turned into such a Parisian icon, is that designer Gustave Eiffel originally proposed to build the structure in Barcelona, but the burghers of that city rejected his plans as too radical. The second is that it was originally thought of as a purely temporary structure to celebrate the *Exposition Universelle*, a World's Fair marking the centennial celebration of the French Revolution; indeed, the specifications for the project insisted that the building should be easy to dismantle.

Yet the tower proved so successful as a tourist attraction and broadcasting station that by the time of its proposed demolition in 1909, when its 20 year "licence" expired – and when this map (see p.180) was published – the City of Paris allowed the Eiffel Tower to remain. Which is not to say that it was universally loved. The tower provoked a storm of opposition from Parisian intellectuals including the novelists Dumas and Guy de Maupassant; Maupassant even took his opposition to the enemy and insisted on lunching in the restaurant every day – on the

Above: Gustave Eiffel. The designer originally proposed to build the tower that holds his name in Barcelona.

Opposite: "Paris. The Exhibition of 1900. View on the Seine". Photographer unknown. Oscar Wilde quipped, "they say that when good Americans die, they go to Paris."

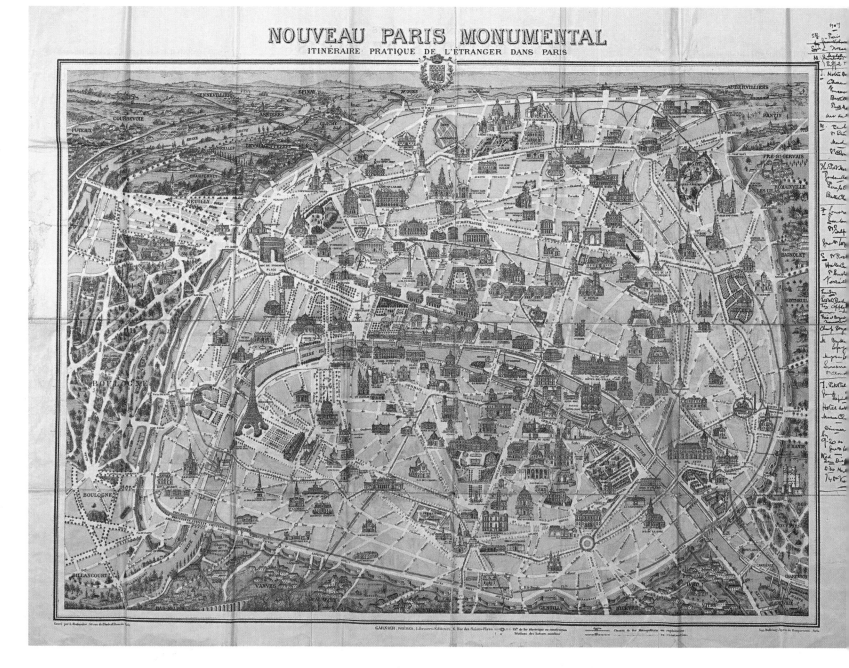

grounds that it was the only place in Paris from which he did not have to see what Dumas had described as "a black blot" on the Parisian landscape with its "odious shadow of an odious column built up of riveted iron plates".

Would any city today necessarily welcome the imposition of such a dramatically high, interlaced iron column on one of its central parks? Perhaps once they had studied the revenue statistics. Over 200 million visits were made up the tower during the rest of the twentieth century, either by the lifts that ascend the three sections or (for the masochistic) the 677 steps.

Gustave Eiffel's original vision was an extraordinarily bold one: to use his experience as a bridge builder to create a tower so aerodynamically shaped as to be capable of resisting the wind, the major risk for a structure that was far from solid –

hence what he described as "the curvature of the monument's four outer edges", which also give the building its elegant and immediately identifiable silhouette.

But Paris could also appeal to visitors for the wealth of its more traditional architecture. The other accompanying map here (see p.181) shows the many cathedrals and churches within reach of the city. It is deliberately wide enough to include to the south-east the greatest of all of these: the Cathedral of Chartres.

The great height of Chartres is exaggerated by the dull plain of La Beauce beside it. The travel writer and poet Sacheverell Sitwell, who was born in 1897, commented on his approach when he could already see the spires from some 12 miles away: "In the case of Chartres no mere comparisons are needed. It seems to exist in a world of its own beside which other names

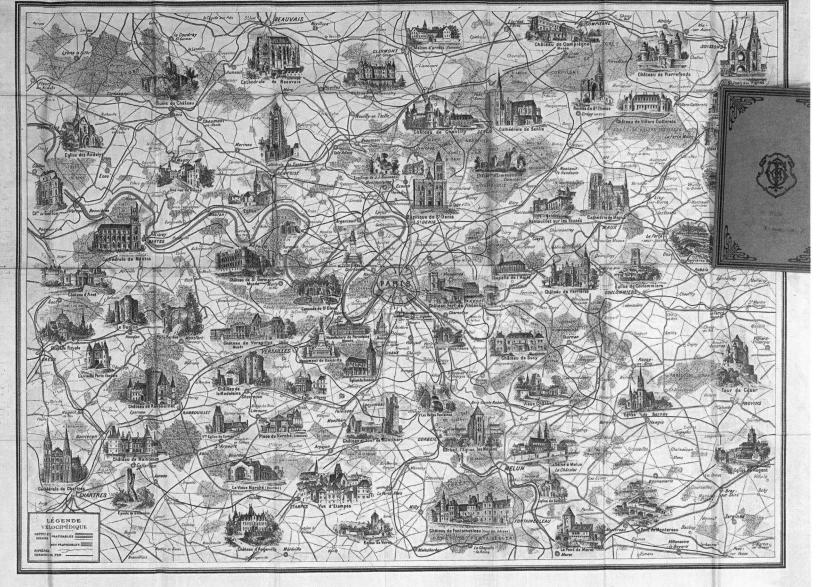

can scarce be mentioned ... it is exceptional and extraordinary."

Like many other great Gothic masterpieces, the construction of Chartres was dogged by fire. After the first cathedral of any great substance burned down in 1020 (prior to this, other churches on the site had also gone up in smoke), a glorious new Romanesque basilica was constructed. Yet in 1194, lightning struck and left only the western end intact, the sole early Gothic section remaining. The rest of the cathedral was built at relatively great speed and with impressive devotion by 1220, the population of Chartres all helping to haul the stone from local quarries five miles away.

There were many innovative features, both architecturally – like the exaggerated flying buttresses – and in the construction. To reach the great heights needed, siege engines known as

Opposite: "Nouveau Paris Monumental: Itineraire Pratique de l'Étranger dans Paris", 1907.

Above: "Monuments et Vues des Environs de Paris", 1907.

Left: Sacheverell Sitwell. He suggested that Chartres, with its elongated architecture, drew in some ways on "an Orientalism of the imagination...".

trebuchets were pressed into service as hoisting cranes. These great slings had been used by both sides during the Crusades, and they were not the only way in which the construction of Chartres was affected by events in the Eastern Mediterranean.

Sacheverell Sitwell made the interesting observation that Chartres, with its elongated architecture, drew in some ways on "an Orientalism of the imagination ...; it is Eastern in ascetic feeling." It is hardly surprising that French Gothic churches should have been influenced by Islamic architecture, given the preponderance of Franks on the Crusades, just as in Spain the closeness of the Moors resulted in Gothic cathedrals like Salamanca having a similarly pronounced architectural debt.

What raised Chartres from the magnificent to the sublime for any visitor was its three rose windows. The supporting flying buttresses allowed far more load-bearing space to be freed up on the main walls, so that stained glass could be used there – stained glass which has remained remarkably intact over the centuries. So the whole of the interior was suffused in a transcendental light. The rose windows contained the vivid blue colour that made Chartres famous and of which Sitwell wrote:

It is in the three rose-windows that the most fiercely burning flames are managed, but above all the blue of sunset and sunrise, miraculously obtained, it is said from seaweed, and obtaining such a blue rose as no other human skill will achieve, or, once attained, will keep alive. It is the clear hyaline of early morning as seen from perhaps thirty thousand feet in an aeroplane, something never seen by previous generations except in the rose-windows.

Chartres was a reminder that Paris and its surroundings, the subjects of these two maps, had always been a place of audacious and intriguing architectural experiment. For any visitor in the early nineteenth century, the Eiffel Tower was just the latest example of this long tradition.

Opposite: "Rue du Rivoli". Photographer unknown, 1900s.

Above: "The Trocadero". Photographer unknown, 1900s.

Following pages: "The Exhibtion of 1900, Eiffel Tower and the Trocadero – Paris". Photograph by E. Hautecoeur, 1900. At the time it was the world's tallest tower, at over 1,000 feet.

The Last of the Windjammers

We were cold and wet, and yet too excited to sleep ... watching the seas rearing up astern as high as a three-storeyed house. It was not only their height that was impressive but their length. Between the greatest of them there was a distance that could only be estimated in relation to the ship, as much as four times her entire length, or nearly a quarter of a mile.

(Eric Newby, *The Last Grain Race*, 1956)

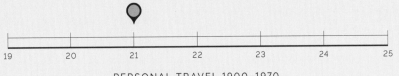

It would be hard to find a more visceral or exciting account of a journey in the twentieth century than that undertaken by Eric Newby (1919–2006), when in 1938 he embarked from Belfast, Northern Ireland, as an apprentice on the four-masted *Moshulu*. He was just 18.

Newby was to find himself part of what had become known as the Grain Race. Old sailing barques would depart from Europe to Australia via the Cape of Good Hope; most, though not all (and this map (pp. 188–89) shows an exception) would then continue around the world and return via Cape Horn, carrying grain they had picked up in Australia.

It was on this homeward-bound leg that they competed with each other for the fastest time, as much out of pride as for economics – although Newby points out that the margin made on such journeys was so tight that the smallest possible crew was used at the lowest possible rates.

Opposite: "Eric Newby with one of the pigs", 1938.

Above: "*Moshulu* taken in Cork (Cobh), June 1936". Photograph by Eric Newby.

Following pages: "Track Chart of the World" with manuscript additions showing the second last trip of the barque *Garthpool* (last British squarerigger) from UK to Australia and back, 1928–29.

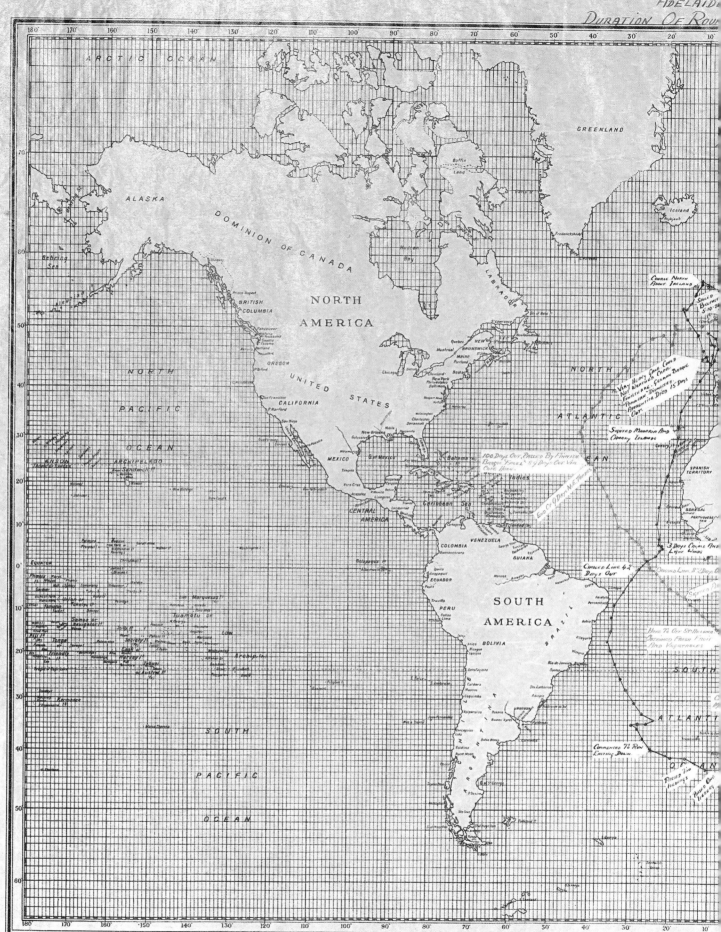

BRITISH SQUARERIGGER   SECOND LAST TRIP

to ADELAIDE   **Sailed** *5ᵗʰ Oct.* **1928** **Arrived** *5ᵗʰ Jan.* **1929** (91 Days. TRACK IN BLACK

QUEENSTOWN & HULL   10ᵗʰ MARCH 1929   18ᵗʰ JULY 1929 (130   TRACK IN RED

9 MONTHS 29 DAYS

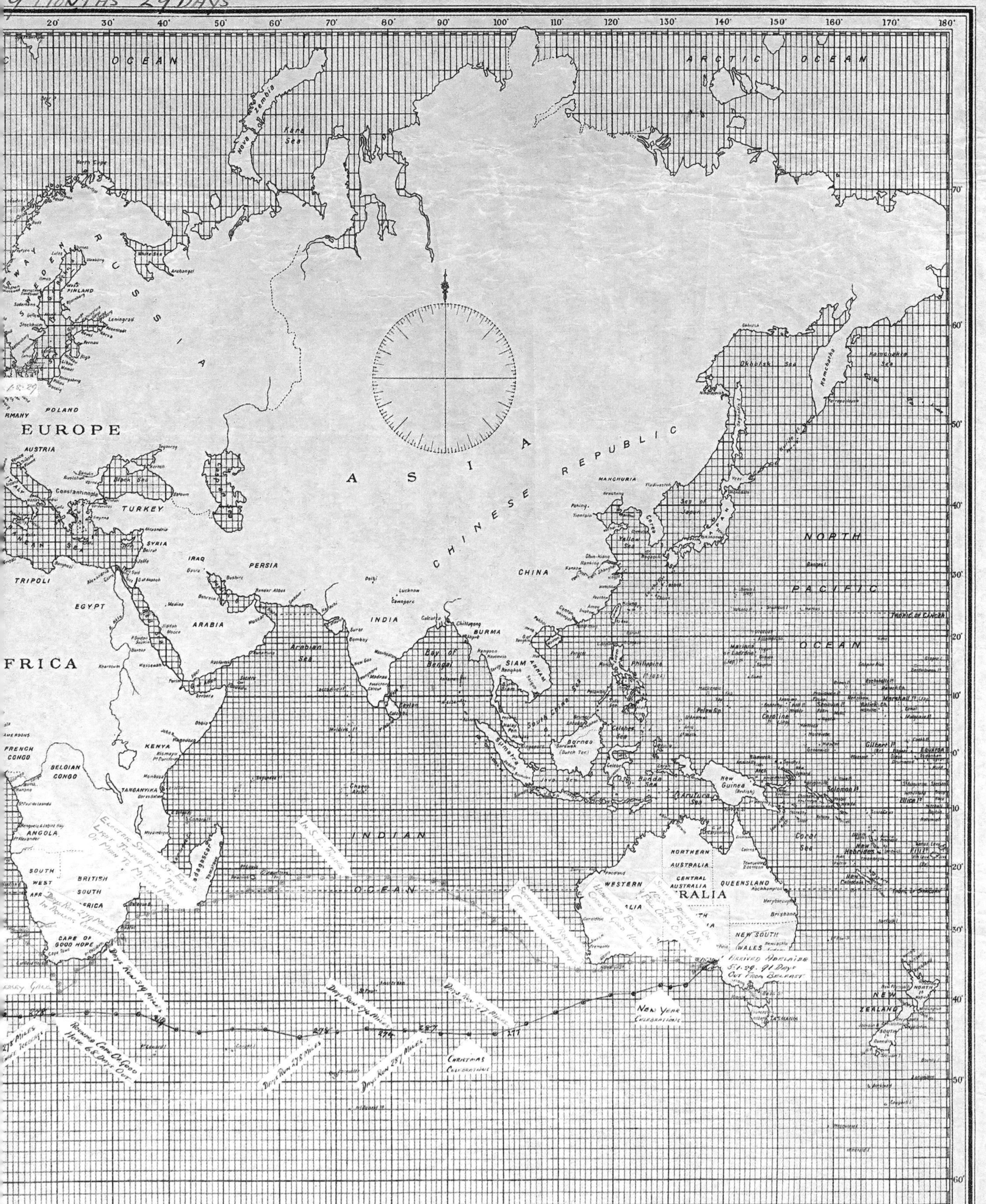

ARRIVED ADELAIDE
5.1.29. 91 Days.
OUT FROM BELFAST

NEW YEAR
CELEBRATIONS

CHRISTMAS CELEBRATIONS

T.H.B. OATES.

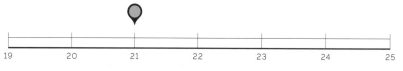

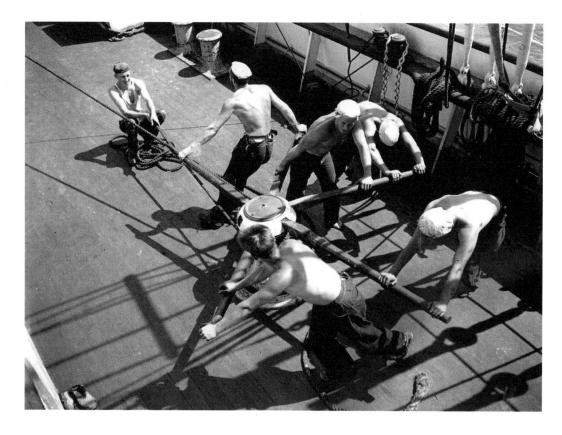

The *Moshulu* was one of the largest sailing ships still transporting grain. For Newby it proved a daunting initiation – and not just when they crossed the equator and his head was shaved and covered with tar in the traditional shipboard manner for newcomers. The hands were expected to go up the rigging in all weathers.

At times they faced ferocious force 11 winds, particularly on the homeward stretch when they were swept by the prevailing westerly winds towards Cape Horn. High seas regularly washed across the decks, forcing the crew to hang onto lifelines. Given that the young Newby's only previous work experience had been as a clerk in an advertising agency, he coped with these conditions with considerable aplomb – despite the fact that most of the crew were either Swedes or Finns, so he had a hard task understanding many of the commands issued to him. The most frequent one was "op the rigging".

At one point he does actually fall (most readers will be surprised that this has not happened before). He describes the way in which he had "no interval for reflection, no sudden upsurge of remorse for past sins, nor did my life pass in rapid review before my eyes. Instead there was a delightful jerk and

I found myself entangled in the weather rigging some five feet below the yard."

Newby published *The Last Grain Race* in 1956, some 20 years after the events he describes, but the vivid quality of his diaries and his photographs already presage the fine travel writer he was to become. Here he is, for instance, climbing high up into the rigging:

> *At this height, 130 feet up, in a wind blowing 70 miles an hour, the noise was an unearthly scream. Above me was the naked topgallant yard and above that again the royal to which I presently climbed ... the high whistle of the wind through the halliards sheaf, and above all the pale blue illimitable sky, cold and serene, made me deeply afraid and conscious of my insignificance.*

On 10 June 1939 *Moshulu* reached Queenstown (as Cobh was then called) in Ireland after a sail of just 91 days from Port Victoria, so winning the Last Grain Race. Newby sensed at the time that he was part of the end of a very old tradition of working ships under sail. The Second World War effectively ended the use of

such craft for commercial shipping. His book is a wonderful elegy for the end of an era.

This map (see pp.188–89) is of peculiar interest. It shows the penultimate voyage of the *Garthpool*, which it names "the last British square-rigger", as it made its journey to Australia and back 10 years before Newby's voyage on a Finnish ship in 1928. She too seems to have encountered some heavy seas. Notes appended by an anonymous crew member show that after being blown off course in the Bay of Biscay, she was unable to weather

Opposite: "Capstan work. Sending a royal aloft". Photograph by Eric Newby, 1938.

Above, clockwise from left: "One of the crew washed into the scuppers", "Strong gale in the Southern Ocean", "A few seconds later. Jumping for the life-line as a big sea comes aboard". Photographs by Eric Newby, 1938.

Cape Finisterre – the same cape which had given the British Navy such problems during the Napoleonic wars. A German barque was completely dismasted in the same storm.

Once they had come far enough south to pick up the westerlies, they could run across the bottom of the Atlantic, passing icebergs as they went, making some fast passages of 300 nautical miles a day, just as Newby was later to do.

Like many a windjammer, they had to wait some time in Australia, both to collect grain and offload ballast, and it was two months before they could leave again for England, choosing to return by the same route rather than the more usual passage via Cape Horn. The map *(see pp.188–89)* shows that after successfully passing through an electric storm off Madagascar, the *Garthpool* had to round the Cape of Good Hope against the full force of the

westerlies and made heavy weather of the Atlantic. She took 130 days to get back to Britain by July 1929, compared to *Moshulu*'s 91. An acerbic note on the map records that north of the Equator they were passed by a Finnish barque, which was coming back via Cape Horn and had already done so in 10 less days than they had.

But disaster was to await the *Garthpool*. Later that same year, when she set off on the next voyage of November 1929, she struck some reefs off the Cape Verde Islands on 11 November 1929. While all the crew survived, the ship never sailed again.

Opposite: "Vytautas Bagdanavicius". Photograph by Eric Newby, 1938.

Above: "Tightening sheets". Photograph by Eric Newby, 1938.

Below: "The wind rose even higher. A lesser ship might well have foundered, but *Moshulu* ran before the storm". Photograph by Eric Newby, 1938.

Travelling the Oceans in Style

There is an archetypal photograph repeated again and again throughout the 1920s. It is of a small huddle of well-dressed locals on the docks of a British port – the men in suits, the women with fur stoles and flapper hats – often holding umbrellas, as it is raining (for the weather could not be rearranged for a ship's launch or day of departure). And they are looking out beyond the docks to the open water, where a magnificent three or four stacked liner, displaying her best lines, is just heading off for the sun and a life of continual gaiety.

It is hard for us now to recreate quite what the luxury ocean liners represented in the period of their heyday from Edwardian times through to the Second World War. Nowadays they are seen as either stately dowagers taking pensioners across the Atlantic, like the remaining Cunard boats, or raucous "booze-cruises" full of thousands of passengers coming out of Miami.

But by the late 1920s and early 1930s, when this map (see pp.196–97) was produced to illustrate the routes of the P&O line, the liners had become extraordinarily graceful and successful. The last liner built for P&O's London to Bombay service, for instance, was the *Viceroy of India*, which would have followed the thick red line through the Suez Canal. This 19,648-ton ship, launched in 1928, had far more first-class accommodation than second-class, as was often typical (415 first-class passengers travelled with only 258 second-class). There were special arrangements so that servants could sleep in rooms just off the first-class suites, and it even had an indoor swimming pool.

But for the last word in luxury style, one had to look to the French. The Compagnie Générale Transatlantique had launched the *Île de France* in 1926. Its Art Deco style caused a sensation and was to prove influential. A widely emulated design feature was the incorporation of a grand staircase that wound down

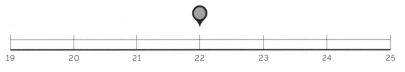

between decks. One can imagine the black-tied passengers from first-class descending first to dine and then dance the night away (as long as they hadn't eaten too well). A ball took place on most nights when the ship was at sea, and well-known dance bands were often contracted to sail on board. Even now, the small luxury cruise boats produced in Italy for modern companies like Silversea and Seabourn are distant echoes of the *Île de France*.

This map (see pp.196–97) deliberately sidelines the Atlantic crossing (and for that matter Britain) to focus on P&O's main routes at the time to India and Australasia. The centre of the map is very clearly the Pacific.

The Peninsular & Oriental Steam Navigation Company had been founded in 1822, first as a shipping line to deliver mail, then from 1844 as a cruise liner travelling on excursions to the Mediterranean. These are thought to have been the first such cruises offered to the general public and so P&O is recognized as the world's oldest cruise line.

However, it was the transatlantic crossings which really developed travel by ocean liner towards the end of the nineteenth century, when the coveted Blue Riband was

EUROPE-AMERICA

Opposite: Swimming "On the *Arandora Star*". Photograph by Alan D. Falk, October 1935. The ocean liners successfully projected an image of a life of sun and continual gaiety.

Above: "Some of the passengers embarking at Immingham Dock", SS *Arandora Star*, 9 July 1932. Photographer unknown.

Left: The Blue Riband prize passed between ships from the Cunard, Hamburg Amerika and White Star lines, all of whom competed for the fastest Transatlantic crossing.

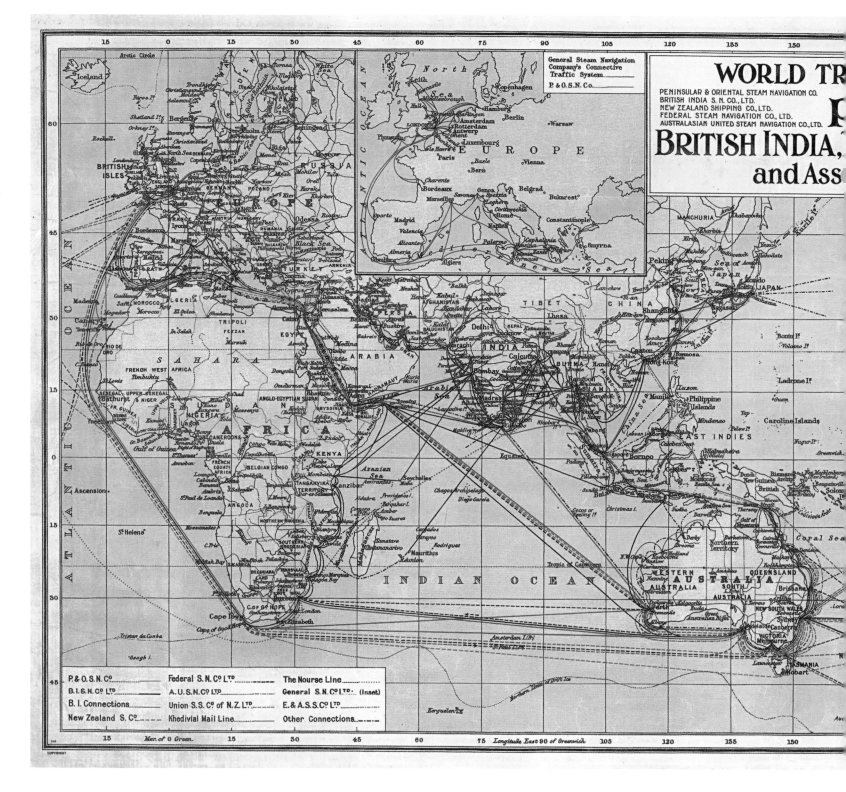

awarded to the ship which made the fastest crossing. By 1900, the 17,000-ton *Deutschland* was awarded the Blue Riband after crossing to New York in just five days, 15 hours and five minutes. The prize passed regularly between ships from the Cunard, Hamburg Amerika and White Star lines, although White Star never recovered fully from the sinking of the *Titanic* in 1912.

Another sinking – that of the Cunard's *Lusitania* by German torpedoes off Ireland in 1915 – contributed to America's eventual decision to enter the First World War, and many German cruise boats were either impounded or scrapped.

But come the 1920s and it was business as usual. Indeed, if anything liners prospered more than ever, and Noël Coward and his friends perpetuated a myth of languid sophistication and sunset romance in which a man in a white jacket was always looking out over the rail, cigarette in hand, as a woman joined him in a cocktail dress. Snappy and witty dialogue would then ensue.

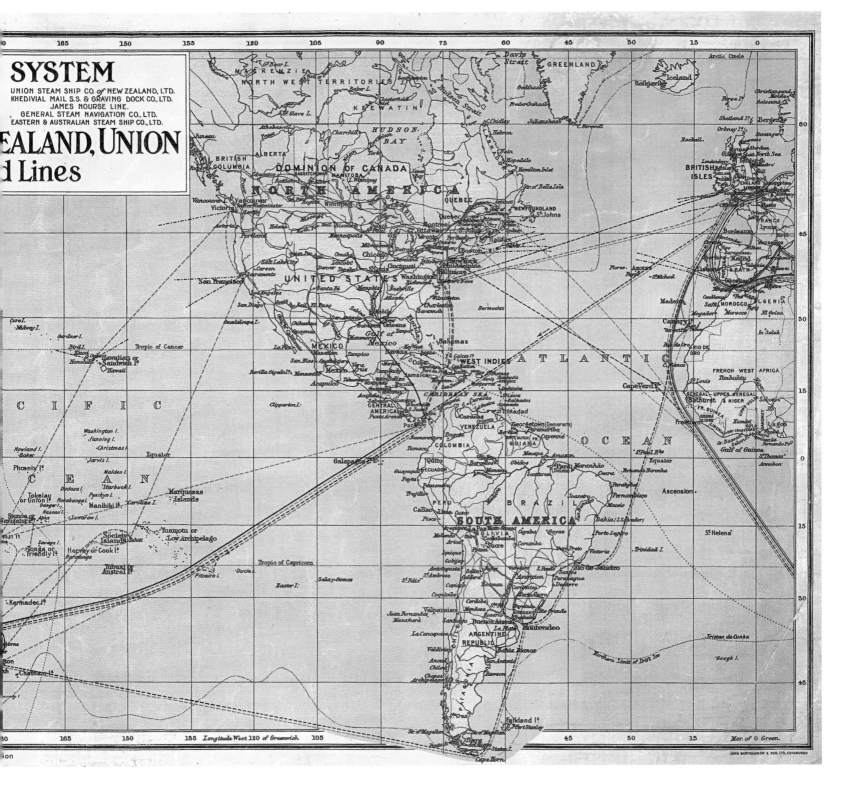

Above: "World Traffic System of the P&O: British India, New Zealand, Union and Associated Liner". J. Bartholomew & Son, 1930.

No longer did the companies try to compete with each other quite so much on sheer size. The accent was more on luxury than speed. So for almost the entire decade Cunard's *Mauretania* – a much-loved veteran from 1906 – held the Blue Riband with an extraordinarily fast crossing of just under four days and 11 hours, travelling at an average of 26 knots. The *Mauretania*'s bar was designed to look like the conservatory of an English country house, with rattan armchairs and bay trees in pots. The bar must have served a lot of drinks, as she could carry 563 first-class passengers and 464 second-class ones. We know, for instance, from the *Titanic*'s cargo list that she sailed with 250 cases of wine, 110 cases of brandy and 192 cases of hard spirits.

This map (see pp.196–97) shows the sheer profusion of routes and choices that passengers could make between different lines. During the 1920s, P&O took delivery of over twenty new passenger liners to add to their already large fleet of almost 500 ships, including those for commercial shipping and mail boats.

The Second World War brought to an end the great age of ocean travel. Many of the liners were commandeered as troop ships or for other purposes. The *Viceroy of India* was sunk after being torpedoed by a German U-boat in the Mediterranean in 1942, although this was after troops had disembarked and so the loss of life was minimal. Overall, P&O lost some 156 of its ships during the war, and the routes to India declined after that country's independence. Although the long-distance routes to Australia continued for some time, given the difficulties involved for commercial flights, the golden age of the great liners was over.

Left: Blue Star Line poster.

Below: *Arandora Star* fancy dress dinner and dance menu, 16 July 1932. Passengers were encouraged to eat well when on board. Then, as now, many left the ship heavier than when they had embarked.

Opposite above: Tug of War "On the *Arandora Star*". Photograph by Alan D. Falk, April 1938.

Opposite below: "*Mauretania* arriving at New York". Photographer unknown, 1920s. For almost the entire decade of the 1920s, Cunard's *Mauretania* held the Blue Riband with an extraordinarily fast Transatlantic crossing of just under four days and 11 hours.

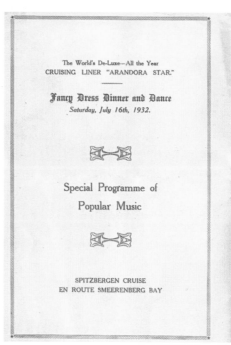

The World's De-Luxe—All the Year
CRUISING LINER "ARANDORA STAR."

Fancy Dress Dinner and Dance

Saturday, July 16th, 1932.

Special Programme of
Popular Music

SPITZBERGEN CRUISE
EN ROUTE SMEERENBERG BAY

Menu

HORS-D'ŒUVRE

Foie Gras in Terrine   Caviar Arandora   Tango Cocktail
Seville Olives   Museau de Bœuf
Eggs Mayonnaise   Fillets of Anchovies   Bismark Herrings
Cod's Roe   Tunnyfish
Pimentoes, Vinaigrette   Celery   Sardines in Oil
Consommé Profiterolles   Potage Mulligatawny
Boiled Scotch Salmon, Cardinal Sauce and Cucumber
Fried Whitebait, Paprika
Chicken in Casserole, Mascotte   Turkey and Tongue Cutlets
Asparagus, Melted Butter
Braised York Ham au Madère
Fresh French Beans   Boiled Rice
Boiled, Roast and Straw Potatoes
Barded English Pheasant, Bread or Cranberry Sauce
FROM THE GRILL (to order):
Tenderloin, Broadway
COLD:
Anglo Ox Tongue   Danish Gammon   London Pressed Beef
Melton Mowbray Pie
Home-Made Brawn   Norfolk Boar's Head
Salad: Lettuce   Tomato   Beetroot   Niçoise
Mayonnaise and French Dressings
Soufflé Paulette
Macédoine of Fruit, Maraschino
Coupe Lakme   Friandises
Savoury: Angels on Horseback   Devilled Almonds
Dessert: Apples, Oranges, Pears, Apricots, Grapes
Assorted Nuts   French Plums
Cheese: Duchess Cheddar   Edam   Cream Gruyère
Camembert   Roquefort   Stilton   English Cheddar
Coffee

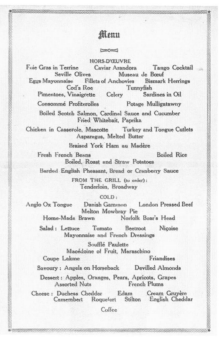

On the Road

*In long-range planning for a trip, I think there
is a private conviction that it won't happen.*

(John Steinbeck, *Travels with Charley*, 1962)

This road-map (see pp.202–03) was produced in 1961. I like to think that John Steinbeck took it in his glove compartment when he decided to travel right across the States for the book that became *Travels with Charley*.

Steinbeck by then was one of America's best-known writers. He was about to win the Nobel Prize. Some of his classic novels like *The Grapes of Wrath* and *East of Eden* had been turned into successful Hollywood movies and were held to be some of the finest twentieth century portrayals of rural America.

But he still felt a need to reconnect with his own country. Aged 60, he decided to travel with his dog, Charley, an elderly poodle, across from the East Coast where he was living to the West Coast, where he had come from, and then back again, doing a large counter-clockwise circuit. The full title of the book, which deliberately copies Robert Louis Stevenson's *Travels with a Donkey*, a favourite of Steinbeck's, is *Travels with Charley in Search of America*.

He wrote to a friend that he wanted:

... to learn about my own country. I've lost the flavor and taste and sound of it. Soooo! I'm buying a pickup truck with a small apartment on it, kind of like the cabin of a small boat, bed, stove, desk, ice-box, toilet ... I'm going alone, out towards the West by the northern way but zigzagging through the Middle West and the mountain states. I'll avoid cities, hit small towns and farms and ranches, sit in bars and hamburger stands and on Sunday go to church ... I just want to look and listen. What I'll get I need badly – a re-knowledge of my own country, of its speeches, its views, its attitudes and its changes. It's long overdue – very long.

The idea of travelling right across the US in this way was in the air. Jack Kerouac had already written *On the Road* (originally typed on a continuous, 120-foot scroll of tracing paper), while Robert Frank's influential book of photos, *The Americans*, first published in 1958, also came out of a long car trip.

Above: John Steinbeck. By the time he wrote *Travels with Charley*, Steinbeck was one of America's best-known writers. He was about to win the Nobel Prize.

Opposite: 1950s family station wagon and trailer, Jackson Lake, Grand Teton Mountains.

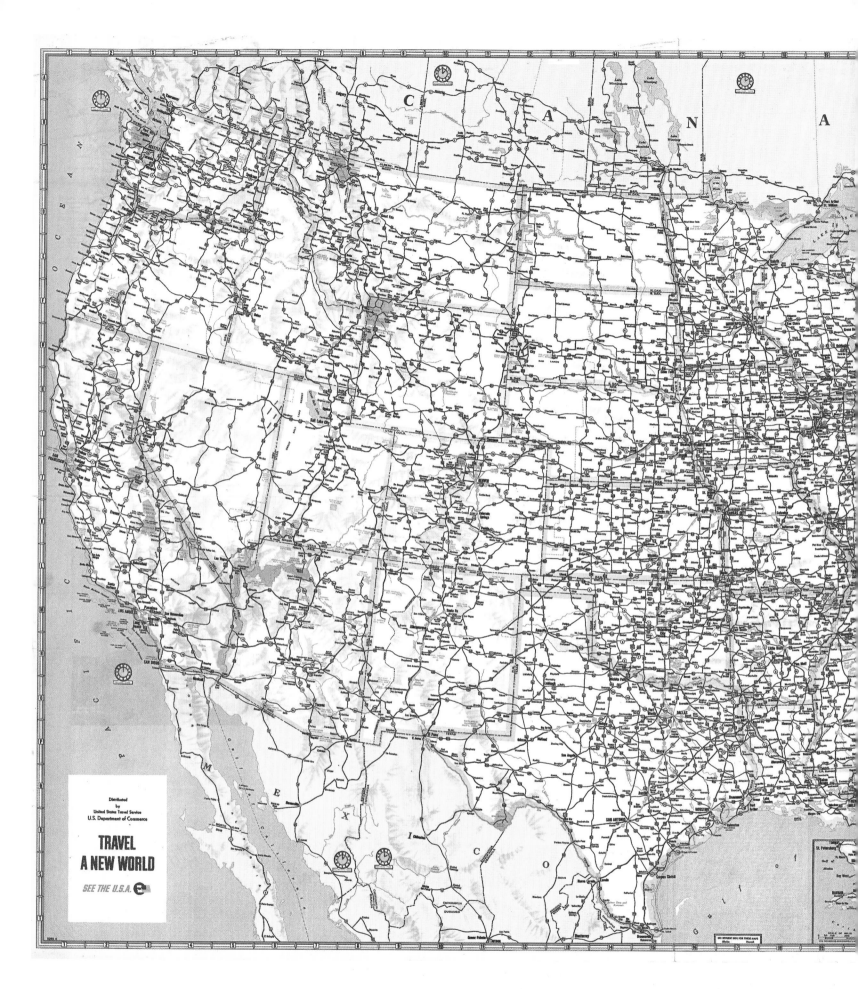

TRAVEL
A NEW WORLD

SEE THE U.S.A.

Distributed
by
United States Travel Service
U.S. Department of Commerce

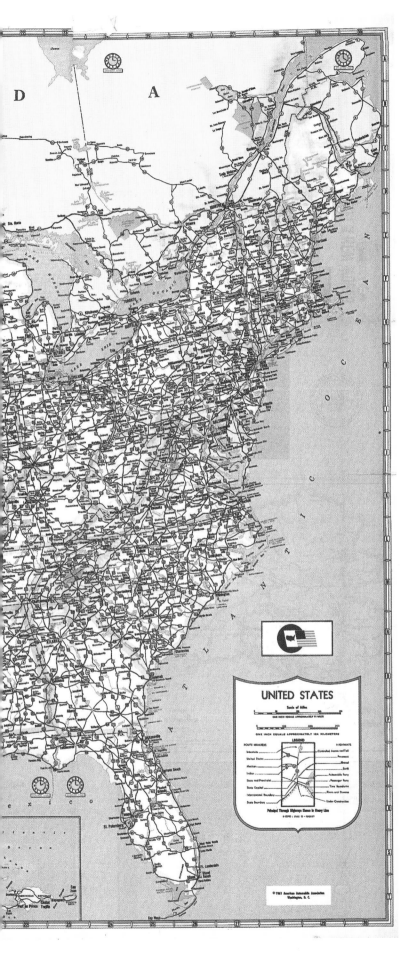

The new highways, as this map (left) shows, had made motoring through the US much easier. Steinbeck, however, chose to take back lanes whenever he could at the start of his journey – before realizing that unless he got on with it, he would never get around the whole country. "Maine seemed to stretch on endlessly. I felt as Peary must have when he approached what he thought was the North Pole." So he used Highway 90 to motor through Ohio and Michigan.

There is a good moment when Steinbeck is heading out of Chicago through Illinois. He describes it as "a noble land of good fields and magnificent trees, a gentleman's countryside, neat and white fenced". But he goes on to make the telling point that it is a subsidized countryside, often lived in by commuters, without "the thrust of land that supports itself and its owner. Rather, it was like a beautiful woman who requires the support and help of many faceless ones just to keep going."

The rise of highways across the US had seen the rise of trailer parks, which fascinated Steinbeck as a new phenomenon: "They are not trailers to be pulled by one's own car, but shining cars long as pullmans. From the beginning of my travels I had noticed the sale lots where they were sold and traded, but then I began to be aware of the parks where they sit down in uneasy permanence."

He was impressed by how elaborate some of these trailers had become. They could be 40 feet long, with multiple rooms and air conditioning. But he was also alarmed at how pervasive they were; someone told him that one in four new housing units in the whole country were mobile homes. It seemed to him an odd symptom of both America's restless rootlessness, but also of its consumerism, for the trailers were full of "all the appliances we live by – dishwashers, automatic clothes washers and dryers, refrigerators and deep freezes".

When he reached the Missouri River in North Dakota, he crossed what he felt was "where the map should fold", the boundary between East and West America. He left the green grass of the east to cross over into what he felt was the pure west, with brown grass and water scorings and small outcrops. Although just a crossing of the river, he said that the two sides might as well be a thousand miles apart.

The journey took him 11 weeks overall to complete. When the book came out, it was a tremendous success. Although

Left: "United States". By American Automobile Association, 1961.

Steinbeck saw very little poverty along the route – and certainly nothing to compare to what he had memorably portrayed as "the grinding terrifying poorness of the 30s" in his famous novels – he had identified a growing disenchantment in America.

But he was also able to reconnect with some its most elemental and iconic landscape, like the redwood trees of California where he described experiencing "a cathedral hush": "Perhaps the thick soft bark absorbs sound and creates a silence. The trees rise straight up to zenith; there is no horizon. The dawn comes early and remains dawn until the sun is high. Then the fernlike foliage so far up strains the sunlight to a green gold and distributes it in shafts or rather in stripes of light and shade."

Travels with Charley was the last major book Steinbeck published before his death in 1968.

This map (see pp.202–03) was produced by the American Automobile Association, which had been founded at the beginning of the twentieth century as motor roads started to carve up the countryside. Service stations would often hand out such maps for free, as a way of promoting more travel and therefore petrol sales. The AAA were some of the principal producers of these maps, along with Rand McNally, and they had helped promote the idea of numbering the highways to make for easier route planning across this vast country.

Although in some ways it can be said that Steinbeck did not want a planned route. He wanted to get lost again in America.

Opposite, above: "US 40 Highway". Photograph from *U.S. 40* by George R. Stewart, 1953. The new highways had made motoring through the USA much easier.

Opposite, below: 1950s heavy traffic, Benjamin Franklin Bridge, Philadelphia.

Above: Trailer park, Hampton Roads, Norfolk, USA. The rise of trailer parks fascinated Steinbeck as a new phenomenon.

Right: 1950s service station attendant filling station wagon.

Below: People relax and talk amid a row of parked campers and trailers at the Wagon Wheel Trailer Park, Maine, late 1950s or early 1960s.

Afghanistan

The Land of Hospitality

We think of Afghanistan as a place that has been ravaged for decades – if not centuries – by war and conflict. But there was a brief period in the 1960s when it opened up to tourists; when, if you were taking the hippy trail out to India, a stopover in Kabul to do some shopping in Chicken or Flower Street was almost mandatory.

During the enlightened reign of King Mohammed Zahir Shah, a political consensus was developed after the Second World War, together with a new liberal sensibility that encouraged women to go to university. This tourist map (opposite) comes from those happier times – indeed it was published in the same year, 1964, as a new constitution introduced free elections, a parliament, civil rights, women's rights and universal suffrage.

Any tourist arriving from the West and Iran would first have stopped at Herat, with its famous minarets and Islamic architecture much praised by earlier travellers like Robert Byron in his classic account of the 1930s, *The Road to Oxiana*. Only the bravest would have attempted to cut across the middle of the country to Kabul; some would have taken the northern route past Mazar-i-Sharif; others, what has now become one of the most dangerous and Taliban-infested journeys on the planet, the southern route past Kandahar. Beyond lay the Khyber Pass and the "magic bus" route out to Pakistan and India through the bazaars of Peshawar and Lahore.

Those that made the detour to the wonderfully named Minaret of Jam, which sounds like something out of an Edward Lear limerick and is prominently featured on the map just east of Herat, would have been well rewarded. The indefatigable

Above: Multi-coloured coat, acquired by Robert Byron in Afghanistan.

Right: "The Musalla at Herat: Mausoleum (*c.*1430 AD) and three of the seven minarets". Photograph by Robert Byron, 1934.

Opposite: "Tourist Map of Afghanistan, Land of Hospitality". Produced by the Information Bureau of the Royal Afghan Embassy, 1964.

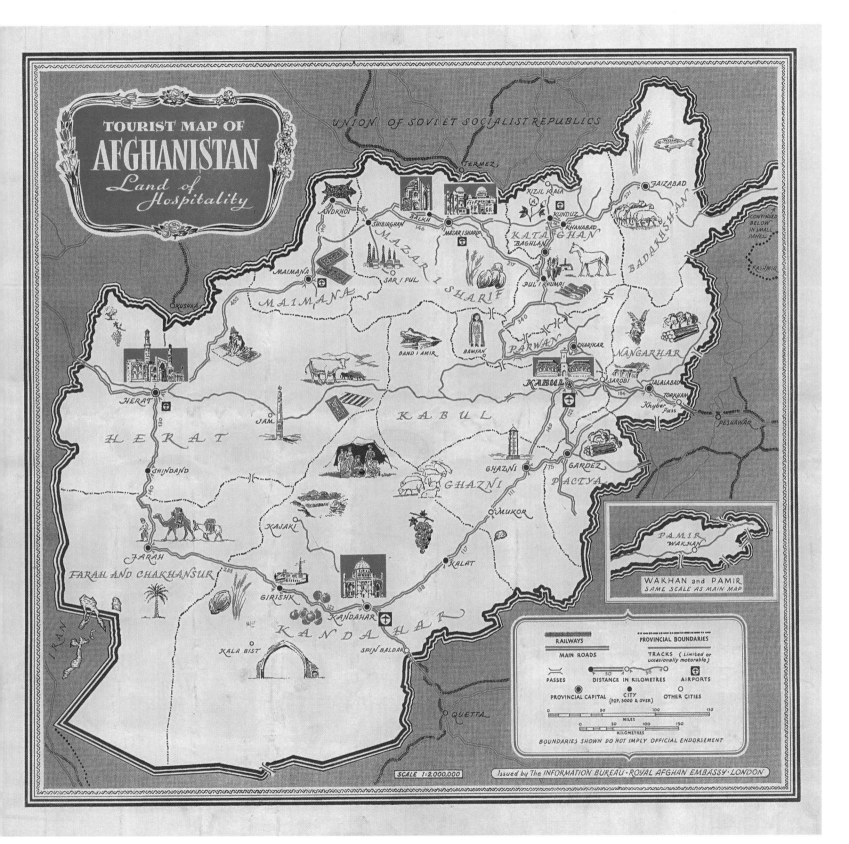

Above: "Putting cud cured lambskins to dry on the roof of a
caravanserai at Andkhui". Photograph by Robert Byron, 1934.

Opposite: Medicine chest carried by Lord Curzon on his
journeys through the Pamirs and Afghanistan.

Freya Stark published a book about the minaret in 1970 (when she was already 77); that same year Peter Levi and Bruce Chatwin travelled there and also extolled its attractions:

> *The minaret is a tall, elegant, shadow-cut, biscuit-coloured pencil magnificently inlaid with turquoise inscriptions, built where its muezzin could best fill the valley with echoes. Seen from below, the obsessional strength of its detail and the depth of its shadows have a mind-blowing power; seen from above, it is a miracle of simplicity and proportion with the rocks.*
> (Peter Levi, *The Light Garden of the Angel King*, 1972)

Standing some 200 feet high and built entirely of brick, the tower is decorated with tiles. The architectural critic Dan Cruikshank has described its shaft as "a dazzling display of virtuoso brickwork, with geometric forms incorporating Islamic eight-pointed stars and Kufic lettering". It has an elaborate set of "double" spiral staircases inside which run contrapuntally upwards and may have helped support the tapering structure through the vicissitudes of earthquakes and floods over the years.

A few brave souls might have followed Eric Newby's example and wandered off to have a "short walk in the Hindu Kush" in the north-east of the country; although they would perhaps have thought better than to venture into Wakhan Corridor, the long awkward finger of land extending to the east that has here had to be appended in a separate box. At the time this map (see p.207) was drawn, there had been no further geographical updates on the Corridor since Lord Curzon's 1895 report for the Royal Geographical Society – an indication of how close to the edge of the known world the River Oxus still lay, just as it did in Alexander the Great's day when he founded the city of Ay Khanoum on the furthest reaches of his empire. Later known as Oxiana, this was a place that attained almost mythical status for later travellers (both Robert Byron and Bruce Chatwin tried and failed to get there).

For despite the cheerful graphics of this map, which imply that visiting Afghanistan was much like visiting Sicily, anyone contemplating taking the hippy trail through the country to India would have needed considerable resourcefulness; Tony Wheeler, the founder of Lonely Planet, famously once managed to hitch the whole journey with just the small change in his pocket.

Of all the travellers drawn to Afghanistan in those years, perhaps the most adventurous was Dervla Murphy, who published her account of her journey through Afghanistan from Ireland in the year that this map was also published, 1964. Born to a family of modest means in County Waterford, Dervla needed to stay at home and care for her invalid parents until she was 30. So desperate was she to travel abroad that when finally able to leave Ireland, she catapulted off to India on a bicycle like, in her own words, "an elastic stretched to breaking point".

Before going, she practised firing a new .25 automatic pistol in the remote Irish mountains. Then she stripped the gears off her trusty bike, Rocinante, so that there was less to go wrong – although that can't have made crossing the Afghan passes any easier. Letters detailing her adventures were posted back to Irish friends in instalments, and eventually became her first and perhaps best-known book, *Full Tilt*.

On that journey through Afghanistan on her bike, Dervla Murphy was appalled to meet other travellers who had never

talked to an Afghan, let alone entered their homes: "All they had done was photograph them." She describes meeting a 25-year-old American boy who she sees as typical of those she met along the route: "For them, travel is more a *going away from* rather than *going towards*, and they seem empty and unhappy and bewildered and pathetically anxious for companionship, yet are afraid to commit themselves to any ideal or cause or other individual."

The map is best seen as a celebration of another time and place when the riches of one of Central Asia's greatest countries had become far more accessible. Afghanistan was never going to become a mass-market destination. But at least in the 1960s you could travel there without needing armed security. There must be many an old hippy traveller who has fond memories of travelling on the "magic bus" route through the country, usually with a carpet or two strapped to the roof.

Left: "Tower of Victory. Erected by the Mahmoud of Ghazni". Photograph by Mr De Cardi, date unknown.

Above: "Buddhist Temple, Bamiyan Valley". Photograph by Lieutenant Colonel F. E. Dun, date unknown.

Opposite, above: "White Marble Mosque at Baber's Tomb, Kabul". Watercolour by G. T. Vigne, 1836.

Opposite, below: "The fortress and citadel of Ghaznee & the two minars". By James Atkinson, 1842.

Following pages: "Tangi Wardak". By Thomas Hungerford Holdich, 1880.

Wainwright's Heartland

The Western Fells of the Lake District

By the 1960s the Lake District had long been Britain's most famous rural playground. And unlike the maps of Wordsworth's time, the mountains were now given pride of place as a principal attraction. But one man was to promote the area arguably as much as the Lake District poets had done in the early nineteenth century.

Alfred Wainwright's beautifully produced volumes have become so iconic – there can be few walkers in Britain who have not held one – we sometimes forget what an extraordinary achievement they were. Hand-written and hand-drawn, these are books made with the love and devotion of a medieval monk; and for Wainwright, his descriptions of each Lake District climb, along with maps and the odd trenchant comment, were worthy of a lifetime's devotion.

   The quality of his draughtsmanship was legendary. He used a special set of 1901 OS maps with the outrageous scale of six inches to the mile to make sure he got every detail right. Having spent the better part of a year on his first guide, he scrapped the lot and started all over again because he wasn't satisfied with the way the right-hand margin was justified. But there is also a quiet underlying wit which has helped many a walker through bog and mist. He also recommended that a walker should carry an official map, like the one illustrated here (see pp.216–17), and not rely just on his books.

   Alfred Wainwright was born in Blackburn, England, in 1907. Despite doing well at school, he left early, at the age of 13, and worked as a clerk, first in Blackburn's council offices and then Kendall's. In 1930, when he was 23, he went to the Lake District for the first time and began what he later described as "a

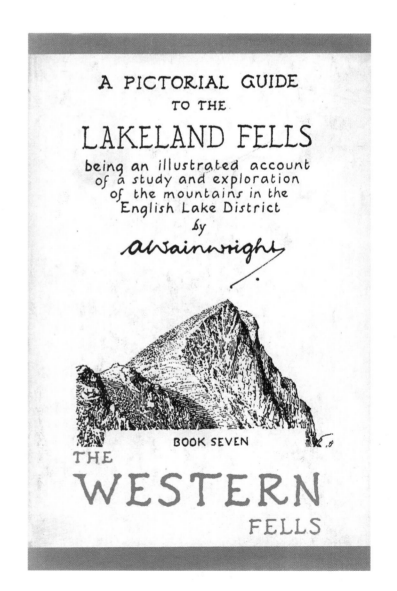

A PICTORIAL GUIDE
TO THE
LAKELAND FELLS
being an illustrated account
of a study and exploration
of the mountains in the
English Lake District
by
aWainwright

BOOK SEVEN
THE
WESTERN
FELLS

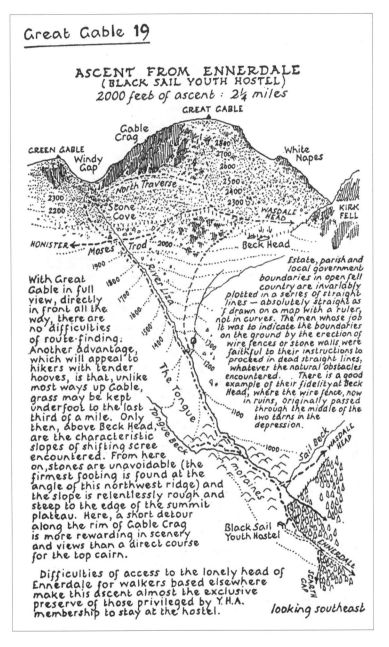

Opposite: *A Pictorial Guide to the Lakeland Fells: Book 7, Western Fells* by Alfred Wainwright, 1966. The last and most personal of his acclaimed series of seven Lakeland books.

Above, left: Alfred Wainwright. When he was 23, he went to the Lake District for the first time and began what he later described as "a love affair with the lakes".

Above: "Great Gable 19: Ascent from Ennerdale". From *A Pictorial Guide to the Lakeland Fells: Book 7, Western Fells* by Alfred Wainwright, 1966. The Western Fells fan out from Great Gable between the lakes of Wastwater and Buttermere.

Left: Cover of "Bartholomew's One Inch Map of the Lake District". By John Bartholomew & Son, 1960. Bartholomew's had a long and distinguished history as a family firm since the first cartographic Bartholomew, George, had worked as an engraver for Daniel Lizars in Edinburgh in the late eighteenth century.

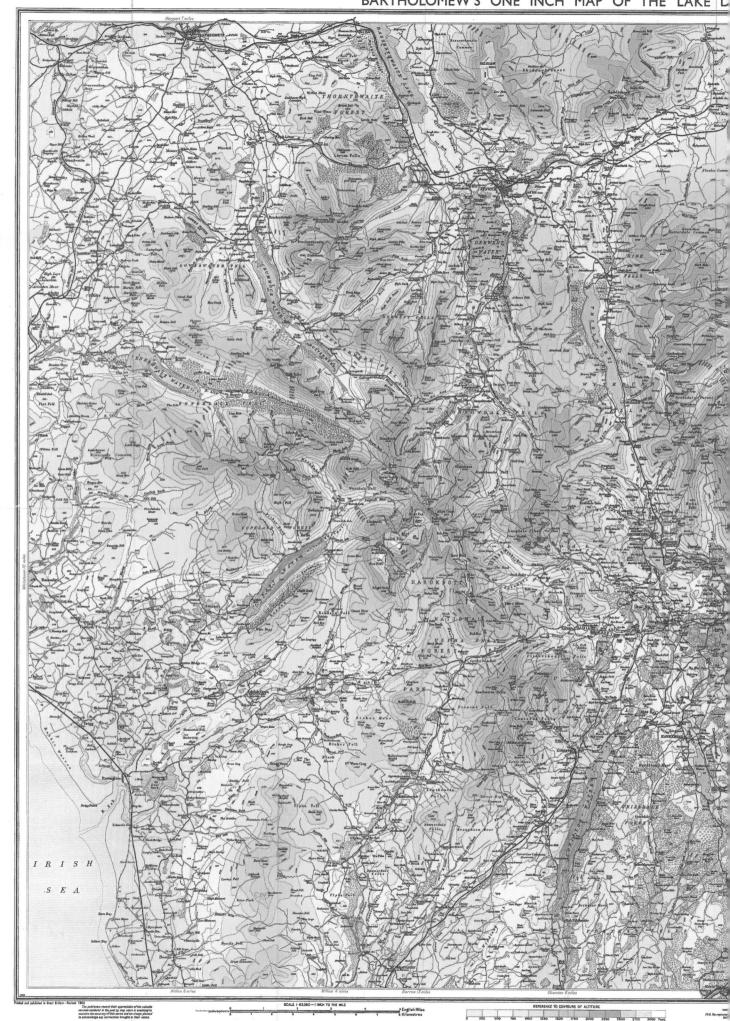

SCALE 1:63,360 — 1 INCH TO THE MILE

REFERENCE TO CONTOURS OF ALTITUDE

0   300   500   700   800   1250   1500   1750   2000   2250   2500   2750   3000 Feet.

English Miles

Kilometres

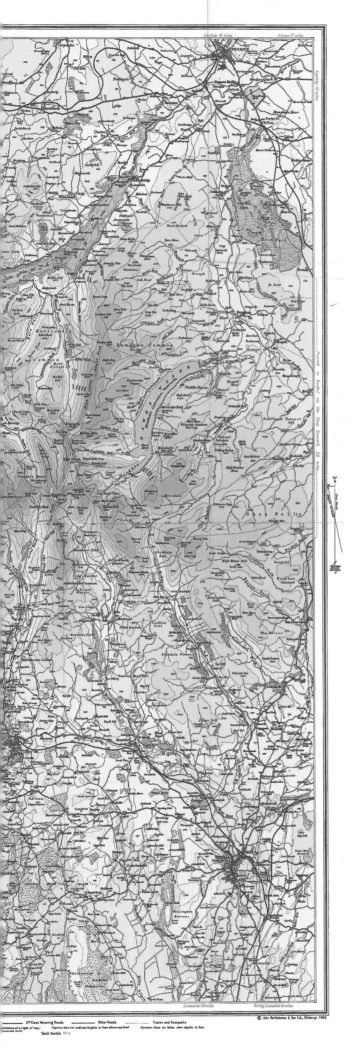

love affair with the lakes", producing a prodigious amount of books celebrating their landscape. He died in 1991.

Nor did he stop at the lakes. He devised and published *A Coast to Coast Walk* from St Bees on the Cumbrian coast to Robin Hood's Bay on the east coast, a walk that has now become one of the most popular in the world.

But however far he wandered, the heartland of the Lake District for Wainwright were these Western Fells, the mountains that fan out from Great Gable between the lakes of Wastwater and Buttermere. It was the area about which he wrote the last and most personal of his acclaimed series of seven Lakeland books ("guides" is surely an inadequate term) in 1966, at a time when he was falling in love with the woman who was to become his second wife; and it is where he chose to be remembered after his death. Not coincidentally, it is one of the least visited corners of the Lakes, furthest from the M6 and the tourist magnets of Dove Cottage and Grasmere. You have to work to get there, and that may have appealed to him. Wainwright did not go into the hills for company.

Of particular delight to Wainwright was the strange geological formation of Haystacks (he always insisted it should be spelled as one word, not, as Bartholomew's have it on this map, two words) that lies at the centre of a great bowl of mountains. This extended plateau commands the valleys of Buttermere and Ennerdale to either side like an enormous

Left: "Bartholomew's One Inch Map of the Lake District". By John Bartholomew & Son, 1960.

Above: "Buttermere Fells". Photograph by John Noble, 1990s.

Blake Fell   1878'

Lamplugh   Loweswater

BURNBANK FELL

▲ BLAKE FELL

▲ GAVEL FELL

● Croasdale

MILES

0   1   2   3

from Cogra Moss

THE SUMMIT

The summit is a small grassy dome with a neat cairn but nothing of interest.

RAISE   WHITE SIDE   ROBINSON   DALE HEAD   ULLSCARF   FLEETWITH PIKE   HIGH RAISE   GREY KNOTTS   GLARAMARA

Buttermere

The bystander, patiently waiting while details are noted but eager to be off, is Barmaid of the Melbreak Foxhounds.

THE VIEW

Principal Fells

The view is better than anticipated, with one aspect in particular, that of Buttermere valley in a frame of fells, of classic beauty.

N

BINSEY · GRAYSTONES · BROOM FELL · LOW FELLBARROW · MELLBREAK (north top) · WHITESIDE · HOPEGILL HEAD · Sand Hill · CRAGMOOR · EEL CRAG · MELLBREAK (south top) and WHANDOPE · WHITELESS PIKE · KNOTT RIGG · MAIDEN MOOR · GREAT DODD · STYBARROW DODD · RAISE · WHITE SIDE

Carling – 5 miles · 10 miles

CARLING KNOTT · BLAKE FELL · GAVEL FELL · Banna Fell · Dent · CRIKE (summit not seen) · GREAT BORNE · CAW FELL · Little Gowder Crag · HAYCOCK · STARLING DODD · RED PIKE · BLACK CRAG · HIGH STILE · PILLAR · SCOAT FELL · ROBINSON · DALE HEAD · FLEETWITH PIKE · ULLSCARF · GREY KNOTTS · HIGH RAISE · GLARAMARA · Broad Crag

W —————— E

S

Lakes and Tarns

N: Loweswater
ESE: Crummock Water (small part of head of lake)
ESE: Buttermere

RIDGE ROUTES: There are no ridges connecting with other fells.

aircraft carrier that has been beached between them. It is possible to wander for hours around its heather-clad knolls and never quite take the same route twice. And wherever you go, you will be afforded a new view of either the lake of Buttermere or Great Gable and some of the other peaks like Kirk Fell and Fleetwith Pike.

At the centre of Haystacks is Innominate or "nameless" Tarn, in the bowl of what Wainwright called "the sunset side"

of the Lakes. That it was a particularly special place for him is clear. In *Fellwanderer*, his autobiography, he made a very public wish to have his ashes scattered:

Opposite: "Gt Gable – the difficult route". Photograph by Michael Spender, 1936.

Above left: "Blake Fell". From *A Pictorial Guide to the Lakeland Fells: Book 7, Western Fells* by Alfred Wainwright, 1966.

Above right: "Hen Comb 4": "The Summit" and "The View". From *A Pictorial Guide to the Lakeland Fells: Book 7, Western Fells* by Alfred Wainwright, 1966.

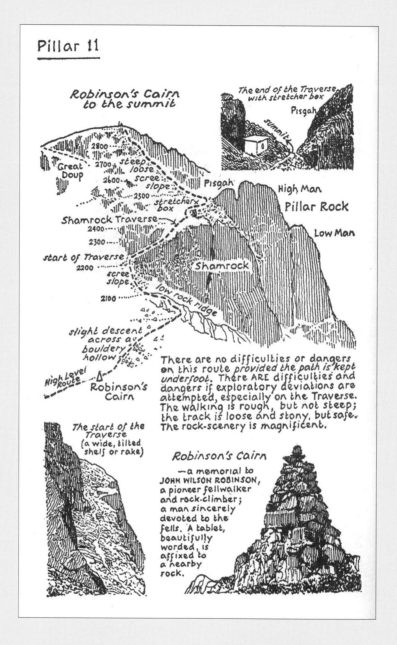

... where the water gently laps the gravelly shore and the heather blooms and Pillar and Gable keep unfailing watch. A quiet place, a lonely place. I shall go to it, for the last time, and be carried: someone who knew me in life will take me and empty me out of a little box and leave me there alone.

He followed this rare statement of emotion with a typically self-deprecating comment: "And if you, dear reader, should get a bit of grit in your boot as you are crossing Haystacks in the years to come, please treat it with respect. It might be me."

The Bartholomew's map illustrated here (see pp.216–17) was of the sort best carried in a plastic sleeve, to be held up and examined in what would often have been driving rain. This is one of the wettest parts of Britain. Seathwaite in the centre of Cumbria (and of this map) holds the dubious honour of being officially England's wettest place, and rainfall levels can be more than two metres a year.

But that would not have deterred Wainwright. He made a point of coming here often, and when he was a young man camped at Stonethwaite for many of his early adventures in the hills.

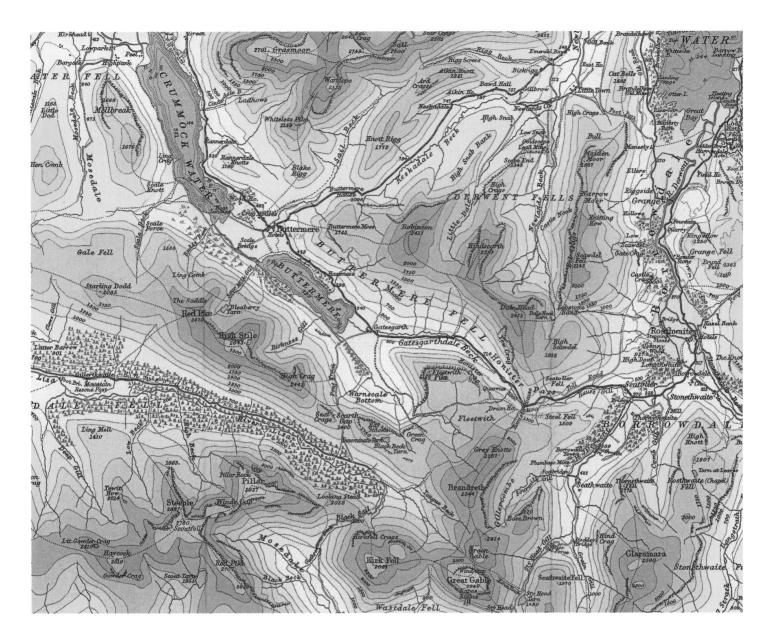

The map illustrated here was one of the last such "one inch to one mile" maps that the Scottish firm John Bartholomew & Son produced, as they later gave way to the stiff competition represented by the Ordnance Survey. The firm had a long and distinguished history since George Bartholomew had worked as an engraver for Daniel Lizars in Edinburgh in the late eighteenth century, and had remained in the same family. One of the maps from their "Commercial and Library Chart of the World" is illustrated above in the article on Hiram Bingham's travels in South America.

Bartholomew's became best known in the latter half of the twentieth century for the *Times Atlas* which they produced and which has become a reference classic. In many ways their history mirrors that of the maps that supplied travellers throughout the whole period covered by this book, as they responded to each new wave of curiosity about the world with cartographic ingenuity.

Opposite: "Pillar 11". From *A Pictorial Guide to the Lakeland Fells: Book 7, Western Fells* by Alfred Wainwright, 1966. The quality of Wainwright's draughtsmanship was legendary. He used a special set of 1901 OS maps with the outrageous scale of six inches to the mile to make sure he got every detail right.

Above: Detail from "Bartholomew's One Inch Map of the Lake District". By John Bartholomew & Son, 1960.

Index

Credits

The publishers would like to thank the following sources for their kind permission to reproduce the pictures in this book.

p44 Scottish National Gallery NG 820, p51 Scottish National Gallery_PG 804, p56t Harris Brisbane Dick Fund, 1948, p60 Private Collection, p148 Public Domain, p150 Chronicle/Alamy Stock Photo, p172, p174, p176b–p178 Granger/REX/Shutterstock. p181b Gordon Anthony/Getty Images, p195b & 198tl Lordprice Collection/Alamy Stock Photo, p200 Bettmann/Getty Images, p201 ClassicStock/Alamy Stock Photo, p202–203 American Automobile Association, p204t ABC-CLIO Greenwood from the book US 40 Highway by George R.Stewart,1953, p204b ClassicStock/Alamy Stock Photo, p205tl Paul Popper/Popperfoto/Getty Images, p205tr ClassicStock/Alamy Stock Photo, p205b Archive Photos/Getty Images, p207 The Embassy of the Islamic Republic of Afghanistan, London, U.K., p214 & p215tr Frances Lincoln, p215tl Topfoto.co.uk, p215bl & p216–217 © National Library of Scotland, p219 & p220 Frances Lincoln, p221 © National Library of Scotland

Every effort has been made to acknowledge correctly and contact the source and/or copyright holder of each picture and Carlton Publishing Group apologizes for any unintentional errors or omissions, which will be corrected in future editions of this book.

Acknowledgements

I would like to thank all the staff of the Royal Geographical Society Collections for their considerable help in the compiling of this book.
In particular I would like to thank Julie Cole, Joy Wheeler and Alasdair Macleod.
I would also like to thank Slav Todorov and Anna Darke, both of whom helped make this book so well, and Jocasta Shakespeare and Patience Thomson for their personal support.

Pr. Patrick I.
Parry Islands
Peninsula
Nth Devon
Baffin Bay
GREENL
Banks Land
Melville Sound
Victoria Land
Baffin Land
Davis Str.
Wrangel I.
Pt Barrow
Arctic Circle
Bering Str.
R. Yukon
Mackenzie R.
Gt Bear Lake
North West Territories
ALASKA
Dawson Klondike
Gt Slave Lake
St Lawrence I.
C. Chudleigh
Hudson Bay
Kamchatka
Bering Sea
Sitka
Peace River Pass
British Columbia
Prince Rupert
Queen Charlotte Islands
DOMINION OF CANADA
Labrador
Quebec to L
Petropaulovsk
Aleutian Is
Vancouver I.
Victoria
Vancouver
C.P.R.
NORTH AMERICA
Chicoutimi
Newfoundlan
St Johns
Quebec
Montreal
Ottawa
Moncton
St John
Miquelon
Nova Scotia
Boston
Winnipeg
Portland
Vladivostock to Vancouver 4401 m.
Yokohama to Vancouver 4320 m.
California
CENT. PAC. RAIL.
Chicago
Mississippi R.
UNITED STATES
New York
San Francisco
Yokohama to San Francisco 4750 m.
Southampton to New
Australasia 6780 m.
2080 m.
S. Diego
STH PAC. RAIL
New Orleans
Charleston
Bermudas
Liverpool
Gulf of Mexico
Bahamas
ATLAN
Cancer
MEXICO
Havana
Cuba
Honolulu
Sandwich Is
Mexico
WEST INDIES
St Thomas
Johnston I.
Acapulco
BELIZE
Jamaica
Haiti
Barbuda
PACIFIC OCEAN
New Route to Honolulu 3830 miles
CENTRAL AMERICA
Caribbean Sea
Barbados
Colon
Trinidad
Marshall Is
Washington I.
Panama
Georgetown
Palmyra
Fanning I.
Cayenne
Gilbert Is
Christmas I.
Arch. de Colon (Galapagos Is)
COLOMBIA
BRITISH GUIANA
Quito
Phœnix Is
Jarvis I.
Malden I.
Guayaquil
R. Amazon
Para
Starbuck I.
Ellice Is
Union Is
Dudoza
PERU
BRAZIL
Solomon Is
Rotumah
Manihiki Is
Marquesas Is
Callao
Lima
Louisiade Arch.
Santa Cruz Is
Samoa Is
Auckland to Honolulu
Auckland to Panama 6578 m.
SOUTH AMERICA
New Hebrides
Society Is
Fiji Is
Paumotu or Low Arch.
Tonga or Friendly Is
Hervey or Cook Is
Sucre
New Caledonia
Ducie I.
Iquique
Jujuy
Asuncion
Pitcairn I.
Caldera
Rio
Brisbane
Norfolk I.
CHILI
Oparo I.
Lord Howe I.
Kermadec Is
Valparaiso
Santiago
ARGENTINE REP.
Montevideo
1281 miles
Buenos Ayres
Rio de la Plata
Auckland
North I.
NEW ZEALAND
Wellington
Valdivia
South I.
Chatham Is
Dunedin
PATAGONIA
Stewart I.
Bounty Is
Wellington to London 11,970 m.
Antipodes Is
Falkland Is
Auckland I.
Campbell I.
Str. of Magellan
C. Horn
Macquarie I.